The Rapala Fishing Guide

Secrets from the Pros

H.R. (Bud) MEIER

It was a labor of love for an avid amateur angler like H.R. (Bud) Meier to assist the authors in editing this book. Bud, who has twice caught Minnesota's largest bass of the year, says he especially liked talking to the pros whose contributions make the RAPALA FISHING GUIDE such a valuable volume.

First Edition

Library of Congress Catalog Card Number: 76-15852

Printed in the United States of America

CONTENTS

IV

DEDICATION

This book is respectfully dedicated to the memory of Lauri Rapala, the originator of the world's most famous family of fishing lures. As he developed his lures, he also quietly began something equally important to the millions of anglers who have found success with those products.

That was the tradition of sharing: *giving freely of himself— advice, encouragement, practical help—to all who ever sought him out. That generosity, which began with the other commercial fishermen in his native Rühilahti, Finland, was extended to anglers all over the world with the distribution of his lures.*

Today, more than 25 million Rapalas have been marketed. They have brought unimagined pleasure to their many users because of the Rapalas' unparalleled productivity in catching all species of gamefish. His lures succeeded from the very start because Lauri Rapala was always a perfectionist, never a "productionist."

He regarded his baits as tools—as perfect as those of any of the other arts or sciences—and he produced them to do a job as perfectly and unfailingly as human design would allow. That job is to catch fish. There is never any compromise with quality. He always had the fisherman's best interests at heart. That tradition is unchanged today.

The purpose of this book is to share, as Lauri Rapala always did, the very latest information on the best ways to use his lures. Our major aim is to increase your fishing success and pleasure. We feel that sportsfishing should, above all, be fun. Fun in fishing means catching fish!

We are confident that this book will add immeasurably to that fun by opening up new angling horizons for you. It was written by some of the world's most successful anglers. We vouch for their techniques. They are now yours for the taking.

(The following message is from Lauri Rapala's sons: Ensio, Risto and Esko Rapala. They continue from where he left off, keeping alive the tradition of careful craftsmanship and quality testing of each individual lure that emerges from the company plant at Vaaksy, Finland.

The letter is aimed at starting the new Rapala user out on the right track in the proper rigging, use and care of these highly successful lures. It is our impression that all Rapala users might read it with some profit, discovering a "do" or "don't" that might increase your fishing success. — The Editors.)

PERSONAL LETTER TO A FIRST-TIME RAPALA USER

Dear First-Time Rapala User:

Because all of us grew up with the Rapala and have been catching salmon, trout and pike with it ever since we can remember, we feel that we might have some insights which will help you in the correct use of the lure. As successful as the Rapala has been in taking all kinds of fish from all kinds of water, there are certain practices to be avoided, others to be encouraged, if you want to start catching fish with it right away.

I. *The first cardinal rule we discovered is to use the lightest terminal tackle possible. And to tie your line directly to the eye of the lure if you can.* If you must use a leader, snap, swivel or combination of these between line and lure, make sure that you use the lightest and finest gear available.

The reason for this is that each Rapala has been individually tested and balanced as it is delivered to you in its box. In hand-carving his earliest models, our father had as his ideal to make the lure as natural and life-like as possible. This meant precision, lightness and balance which, when put into motion, would yield the most natural simulation of a swimming baitfish ever discovered.

It stands to reason, then, that most of this attention to precision will be destroyed by hanging the lure on anything that would impair the balance and precision: i.e., a heavy wire leader or an assortment of weights, snaps and swivels that would cause it to run less than true.

True, it sometimes may be necessary, particularly with the larger models, to use some intervening tackle when retrieving at unusual speeds and depths or seeking a fish that would make short work of a non-metallic leader. In these cases, make the strictest compromise possible in favor of life-like action.

II. *The second cardinal rule involves the use of weight: keep additional lead and sinkers at several minimum distances ahead of the Rapala to reduce interference with the built-in action:*

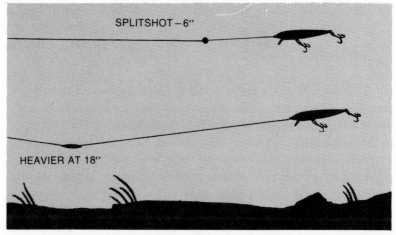

1.) The smallest weights, tiny split shot, can be as close as 6 inches to the lure, but no closer.
2.) Larger weights should be at least 18 inches up the line or leader.

When using three-way rigs involving extra weight, all of the writers in this book recommend at least 18 inches of mono or line between swivel and lure. Several recommend much more, and for good reason: weight close to the natural eye of the Rapala impedes action as much as extra snaps and swivels.

If you need extra weight to get down to where the fish are, there is a companion weighted model for each of the floating Rapalas. Therefore, use a sinking Countdown model to achieve the desired depth rather than using lots of heavy hardware with the similar floating model. The same is true of the sinking Magnum models. We also offer the Deep-Diver which floats at rest but dives to depths of 20 feet on fast retrieve.

III. *The third cardinal rule pertains to the action of the lure: Before you use your Rapala for the first time, we recommend that you check its action, from the boat or a dock, so you can visually confirm the best speed and rigging to give it the most life-like swimming action.*

If you have used weight and line properly, the only other variable to be concerned with is speed. As you watch, vary the speed of the retrieve, noticing that there is an optimum rate at which the Rapala looks exactly like a bait fish scrambling for its life! This is a good speed to adopt when you begin fishing. Of course, as you gain in experience and confidence, you might want to vary the speed, modifying the action for certain conditions and species. But, generally, the Rapala catches gamefish like no other artificial lure because it imitates baitfish better than any other. Note, too, that there are speeds above and below which the lure is not effective. Neither a motionless nor a broaching plug will do the job it is designed to do.

III. *A corollary to rule number three is that when trolling, slowly play out the Rapala from the boat, keeping visual contact with the lure for as long as you can to make sure that it is trailing properly with the correct action.* This visual check will also allow the skipper to find the correct trolling speed for optimum action. If you are trolling near vegetation, pick up periodically to make sure that no bit of weed is impairing your action. The Rapala is too perfectly balanced for hitchhiking debris.

IV. *Cardinal rule number four deals with the care and handling of your Rapala. It deserves special consideration because of its precision balance and the basic material from which it is manufactured.* As innovator of the now-immense family of "pencil" type lures, our father ultimately selected balsa as the wood for the plug body after much experimentation.

Balsa is light. It gave him the specific gravity in the finished product very close to actual forage fish. But balsa is also soft. Because of its precision and balance, please do not use the Rapala as a "handle." You'll probably catch lots of fish with it. But don't use the lure to lift your fish into the boat. Land your fish by hand, in a net or with a gaff. But always spare your Rapala any undue strain. Also use care in removing your catch from the mesh of a landing net. A twisting, turning fish with a Rapala still firmly embedded in its mouth can easily damage the lighter hooks when they are anchored in the net.

Also understand that the Rapala probably has the world's sharpest hooks! They are custom-made with needle-like points. Designed to catch fish, they've also been known to snag unwary fishermen. So please use common sense. Be careful of your fishing partners and yourself; then you'll be able to keep your lure in the water and ready for the nearest fish. We also suggest carrying a small pair of needle-nose pliers or a Hook-Out disgorger to help free the lure from fish.

The fifth and final cardinal rule for fishing with your new Rapala concerns knots: jam-knots vs. loop-knots and when and how to use them when connecting up your Rapala.

As the illustration indicates, the major difference between these two kinds of knots is self-evident: the jam-knot keeps the line snug and tight up against the eye of the lure. The loop-knot permits freer movement between line and lure.

V. *The fifth rule is this: Do not use a jam-knot unless you are trying to control the action of the Rapala. Do use a loop-knot when you want your Rapala to perform more freely and spontaneously.*

In practice, the experienced fisherman will probably use a jam-knot. This allows him to control or vary the action of the lure, usually exaggerating the normal swimming action for surface fishing or very slow trolling. However, in normal fishing applications, use one of the loop-knots. For detailed instructions on how to tie them, turn to Bill Cullerton's chapter on knots in this book. Loop-knots give the lure a wider latitude to move when precise control is not as important as in the examples cited above.

With the Rapala, as in all other kinds of fishing, knowledge and confidence come with experience. If you observe the do's and dont's outlined in this letter, we are sure that you will avoid some of the pitfalls that have slowed the development of other fishermen.

UNI KNOT

1. Run the line through the eye for at least 6 inches. Fold it back to form a double line and make a circle back toward the hook or lure with the tag end.

2. Make six turns with the tag end around the double line and through the circle. Holding the double line at the point where it passes through the eye, pull the tag end, as indicated by arrow, until the six turns are snugged into a tight barrel.

3. Now grasp the standing part of the line and pull (see arrow) to slide the knot up against the eye.

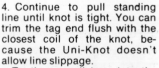

4. Continue to pull standing line until knot is tight. You can trim the tag end flush with the closest coil of the knot, because the Uni-Knot doesn't allow line slippage.
   To tie a small loop into the eye of a lure or fly, giving it free movement in the water, tie the same knot, up to the point where the turns are snugged up around the standing line.

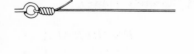

5. Next, slide the knot toward the eye of the lure, by pulling on the standing line, until the size loop desired is reached. Use tacklebox pliers to hold the knot at this point, pulling the tag end to maximum tightness.
   Under normal casting and retrieving the loop will hold. Once a fish is hooked, the knot will slide tight against the eye for better security.

JAM (CLINCH) KNOT

A good knot for attaching snaps or swivels or when tying directly to lure, is the clinch knot.

1) Start by inserting end of line into wire eye of lure and doubling it back against itself. Make 5 turns with the loose end around the standing part of the line.

2) Pass the end between eye of lure and first coil.

3) Next, slip the end back through the loop that has been formed and slowly pull tight.

On the other hand, we have learned much from reading the following chapters. We know you will share our excitement as you read on. That is the beauty of fishing. There is always something new to learn. And there is always a new thrill waiting, on the next cast or at the next bend in the river.

Very Sincerely Yours,

ENSIO RAPALA
RISTO RAPALA
ESKO RAPALA

RON WEBER

A University of Minnesota graduate with a quarter century of experience in the fishing tackle industry and a world-class sport fisherman, Ron Weber brings a multitude of talents into focus in his position as president of Normark Corporation, the Minneapolis-based company that introduced Rapalas to the grateful anglers of the western world.

As he relates below, Ron first encountered definite word of the legendary (and originally elusive) Rapala while on a fishing trip back in 1959. The rest is history. Today, he continuously tests the lure and its refinements on the major species of fresh and salt-water gamefish: from the rare shee fish of the Arctic to tarpon, snook and the wahoo of the tropics and the bass, trout and walleyes of his native regional waters.

The trophy he prizes most is a 14 pound Minnesota walleye: taken on a Rapala, of course. Below, Ron Weber gives some basic directions for using the world's largest selling fishing plug, with more than 25 million marketed since that fateful Canadian fishing trip back in 1959.

THE LURE FISH CAN'T PASS UP

During the late 1950's, while traveling northern Minnesota and Wisconsin as a regional manager for a large fishing tackle manufacturer, I began hearing rumors of a lure from the "old country": a lure so effective and hard to come by that individual plugs were often sent as gifts from friends and relatives in Finland, or purchased on trips abroad.

I was partially skeptical, but not completely so, because most of the successes were attributed to old Finns, or "Suomalainen", who brought with them an abiding love of angling when they migrated to the Uppermidwest at the end of the last century. Therefore, I was willing to listen, when, in the spring of 1959, I stopped off in Duluth to see my friend, George Balmer, while on my way to Canada for an Ontario fishing holiday.

Half-kiddingly, he asked: "What the heck are you going all the way to Canada for? You should stay here and fish with my neighbor. Almost every night he goes across the road to Pike Lake and trolls the weedline for walleyes. He usually comes in with a limit. Some up to eight, nine pounds. He really kills the big ones!"

When I asked the next, inevitable, question, I wasn't overly surprised when George replied: "Oh, that Finnish lure. I think they call it the Rapala."

This was the first direct reference I'd heard made to the lure which would truly revolutionize angling through its unique, lifelike action and ability to capture all species of gamefish. However, my fishing trip to Canada was planned, so I proceeded to Gull Wing Lodge near Dryden, Ontario, to meet my good friends, Bill Smith and Al Wallin, who owned and managed the lodge. Gull Wing and the many surrounding lakes provide excellent fishing. Producing a very respectable limit of fish on most days would not be a problem. Yet, our first day of fishing did prove to be disappointing with only a few very average-size fish being taken. The weather was unseasonably hot, very calm and the lake seemed dead.

I was pleased the next morning when one of my resorter friends suggested we portage over to an adjoining lake to catch some walleyes. This adjoining lake was one of those "can't miss" lakes, full of two to five-pound walleyes with an occasional northern pike over 20 pounds to spice up the action. Yet, by the middle of the afternoon of that day, our results were disappointing. Only a few scattered walleyes had shown and it was anything but exciting fishing.

It appeared the second day of the trip also was going to be a bust. About that time, my friend reached into his tackle box, commenting that he hated to chance losing the last of his precious lures, but he *had* to get serious about his fishing. It seems our catch for that day was to provide a fish-fry for the whole camp the next night. His hand emerged from the confines of his ample tackle box, cradling his last remaining Rapala like a real gem. This was my first glimpse of that mysterious and elusive Finnish lure that would change my ideas about fishing and ultimately change my whole career. What I was to witness in the next hour was one of the most amazing fishing experiences one could imagine.

Returning to the same waters that had produced virtually nothing for the entire day, my friend immediately began producing one walleye after another, trolling his precious last Rapala. Virtually every time we would pass over the tumbled rocks of a previously fishless point, he would get a strike and land another fat walleye. Now I am not used to being out-fished so badly in my native northern waters, so I began changing lures from one "old favorite" to another. I tried varying techniques, adding sinkers to get deeper, removing sinkers to go shallower, pumping the rod to give the lure action, letting out more line to get further behind the boat's wake—all to no avail.

A little balsa minnow from Finland out-fished me on every turn and made a real believer of me that afternoon. And, if that weren't evidence enough, upon returning to camp, a guest was

4

proudly displaying a limit of husky lake trout he had taken that day. After much evasion, he confided to me over drinks later that evening that he, too, had filled out with a Rapala by casting to the reefs and rock piles in Gull Wing Lake. It is no wonder that by this time I really had a case of "Rapala fever" and could hardly wait to get my hands on a quantity so I could get in on this fishing bonanza. I was able to learn from these reluctant anglers that there was a very small quantity of these lures available in Duluth. The trail led back to Dove Clothing Store owned by Alex Kykkonen, the Finnish Consul in that Minnesota port city, who sold some imported specialty items among his selection of work clothing. The few Rapalas I purchased proved to be every bit as good as the rumors I had heard and the results I had observed.

The Rapala obviously had that basic ingredient so necessary in every lure that is to become a standard: that is, it consistently caught fish. This certainly had to be a lure that the American fisherman would welcome to increase his success. So, I wrote the manufacturer in Finland and placed an order for 500 lures for distribution in the Minnesota area. They arrived early in 1960 and, as anticipated, sales took off immediately. They sold only on the word-of-mouth advertising among successful anglers. This was no surprise to me as I knew what the lure could do—consistently catch fish.

In the meantime, I decided to join forces with Ray Ostrom. Ray was a customer of mine in my fishing tackle business and a good fishing friend who owned and managed his own store, Ostrom's Marine & Sporting Goods in Minneapolis. Ray was as eager and enthusiastic as I was when he had a chance to fish the Rapala. As two fishing buddies many times do, we started out on a very loose partnership, on a financial shoe string, and with a great deal of optimism. Not that we were completely inexperienced, since Ray was well versed in the retailing of fishing tackle and I had a good background in distribution and wholesaling; yet, our most important asset was our enthusiasm and blind faith concerning Rapala Lures. The business went well the first two years. We sold all the production the Rapala family and their neighbors in Riihilahti, Finland, could produce. Our venture was off to a good start and it appeared that we were establishing a nice small business with good potential for long-term growth.

What happened next to our friendly little partnership was beyond imagination. We were completely unprepared when the August 17, 1962, issue of LIFE Magazine hit the newsstand with an article entitled "A Lure That Fish Can't Pass Up." You guessed it! That lure was the Rapala. As if good fortune weren't kind enough in merely printing the article, that particular issue of LIFE turned out to be one of the all-time best-sellers. It was the now-famous Marilyn Monroe issue. It was like pouring gasoline on a campfire . . . a flare-up that resulted in a backlog of orders for over three million lures! Many of the orders were prepaid, the frenzied anglers stuffed cash in envelopes with plaintive notes begging for as many Rapalas as the remittance would cover.

Enterprising Rapala owners began renting the lures for $5 a day with a $20 deposit! It sounds incredible now thinking about it, but it is absolutely true. The mania was reaching such heights that black marketeers demanded and received up to $25 per Rapala; and, of course, the lucky few who obtained the lures and went fishing with them were producing unbelievable catches of fish. There was no way we could meet the demand. I had heard of such dilemmas, but couldn't believe it until this time. Business was too good. Rapala and our little company had gone national in the big leagues overnight and, of course, there was no way we could deliver.

Our business with the Rapala family for the first two years was entirely by mail. Very little correspondence, in fact, resulted. When I finally met Lauri Rapala and his family in 1962, he proved to be a quietly courteous commercial fisherman who was forced to use his wits during the worldwide depression of the Thirties. In his humble, genuine way, he explained that those hard times, plus governmental restrictions on the netting of fish, had made it imperative that he devise an artificial lure to provide both income and food for the table and his growing family in the village of Riihilahti, Finland.

"I whittled my own lures and even forged a lot of my own hooks," he told us through an interpreter. "In those lean days,

I didn't have enough money to buy even the plain hooks, let alone lures."

But Lauri Rapala had plenty of time to observe the behavior of minnows and other forage fish as he plied his home-crafted lures with a hand line from his row boat. "I used to stop rowing from time to time to rest or eat my lunch," he once told me. "In the clear lake waters, I would watch schools of minnows swarming under the boat. These minnows would be passing over predator fish for long periods of time, the predator apparently paying no heed. Suddenly, from the literally thousands of minnows overhead, the predator would dart into the school and engulf a victim.

"I began to wonder, was it just by chance that that particular minnow became his meal? Why not the minnow closest to the predator fish? Many times the victim selected was one of the most distant minnows in the school. What distinguished this victim from the thousands of other potential forage fish who many times would be ignored for hours? After years of observance and questioning, I finally began to detect a pattern evolving. There really was reason and logic as to how the luckless minnow was selected. Nature was repeating herself in her wondrous way, winnowing out the weaker of the species.

"The minnows struck by the gamefish invariably were those that appeared slightly abnormal in their manner or rhythm of swimming. This difference most times was so miniscule that it was only after years of observing and training my eye that I was able to detect the difference. Was the victim genetically not perfect? Perhaps slightly wounded? Whatever the difference, it was so slight that only the very closest observation would result in detection. But the pattern was there. After some time, I became so adept in observing these clouds of minnows that I could predict which minnow would be the next victim, when a large fish decided to feed. Out of the dozens, hundreds or thousands of minnows in a school, the difference truly was detectable. This slight variance in swimming action became the basis for the design of my lures from that time forward. This action is what I tried to achieve in my early days of whittling pine bark and balsa. This is my 'secret' which has made my lures successful in catching fish."

Thus, Lauri's keen sense of observation, plus his skill and patience with a carving knife, led to the design of a lure with the most lifelike swimming action ever devised. His selection of pine bark and, ultimately, balsa wood as the basic material gave his lures a buoyancy that permitted them a more delicate, quivering action than some denser, heavier materials would allow.

To assure that authentic, lifelike action, Mr. Rapala carefully tested each lure for balance and movement in a stream near his home, making any fine adjustments that might be necessary.

First Lures Were Made Here

Such meticulous attention to detail led to a clearly superior bait. Soon, word of the large catches he was making spread throughout the village and other fishermen began asking to buy his lures.

This had led, by the time I arrived in Riihilahti, to a considerable "cottage industry", with Mr. Rapala, his four sons and members of their families carving and assembling the lures in strict accordance with the procedures established by the originator.

Today, production has been vastly increased and occurs in a modern plant in Vaaksy, Finland. It employs some 150 townspeople. The founding tradition is still observed: each lure is handtested by a trained craftsman to see that there is no deviation from the uncompromising standards of Lauri Rapala.

Normark Corporation principals Ron Weber, left, and Ray Ostrom proudly display the award presented them, on behalf of satisfied fishermen all over the world, by the Rapala family on the occasion of the marketing of the 25 millionth Rapala lure.

The award, a silver plaque decorated with a Rapala lure, was presented in 1975 in Finland by the Rapala family, descendants of the late Lauri Rapala who invented the world-famous lure. Family members still operate the business. Each lure is individually tank tested and carefully balanced to the highest standards of the Rapala family.

Ron Weber, Normark president, said, "The award was both a surprise and an honor. We have had an excellent relationship with the Rapala family through 15 years. Proof of that, I guess, is the number of Rapala lures sold to date: 25 million."

Normark secretary-treasurer Ray Ostrom said, "We thank the nation's fishermen for the success of Rapala lures."

The happy users of 25 million Rapalas second those sentiments: thanking the Rapala family and Normark Corporation for "The Lure Fish Can't Pass Up."

Triumphant angler emerges from Finnish lake holding trophy 31-pound northern pike captured on Rapala. Lauri Rapala found secret of artificial lures by observing predators like this selecting and capturing natural baitfish.

Ensio Rapala, one of Lauri Rapala's sons and Managing Director of the family-run business, holds 45-pound Atlantic salmon taken from the Teno River on the lure his father perfected.

*Another of the inventor's sons, Plant Manager Risto Rapala, holds a huge
Atlantic salmon caught in river in Lapland on a family lure.*

Esko Rapala, Technical Director of family-run business, and a large northern pike. The Jointed Rapala that hooked and held it is still fast in the northern's jaw.

Normark Corporation corporate headquarters in suburban Minneapolis, Minnesota, at 1710 East 78th Street, Richfield, MN, 55423

Normark, Ltd., of Canada, 1257 Clarence Avenue, Winnipeg, Manitoba, Canada, R3T IT4. Its companion company (not shown) is Normark Sports, Ltd., 32A Chapel Street, Buckfastleigh, Devon, TQ 11 DA Q, England.

Normark Scandanavia, AB, Post Office Box 88, Malung, Sweden.

Rapala Factory. Rapala-Uistin, Vaaksy, 4, Finland. It is here that Rapala lures are manufactured for world-wide distribution.

Stu Apte-hooked tarpon rears angrily from waters of the Florida Keys, trying in vain to free a Rapala lure from its bony mouth. Superior sharpness is hallmark of Rapala hooks.

Each Lure is Tank-Tested and Balanced to this Day

Mr. Rapala, as the dedication of this book indicates, died in 1974 at the age of 68, but his spirit lives on in the workers' commitment to the tradition of quality and craftsmanship he inaugurated almost 40 years ago. The future growth of his lures will always be limited by the demands of handcrafting, despite the incorporation of the latest improvements in plastic lip material, reinforcing wire, metal foils and coating films. There will never be any short-cuts in material and workmanship; each lure will always be hand-tested before shipment to make certain that the swimming action Lauri Rapala so painstakingly researched and designed into his minnows is always retained.

I have caught scores of gamefish on Rapalas, even saltwater roosterfish which, theretofore, had been taken only on live bait.

From this point of vantage, I would like to offer two valuable suggestions about fishing your Rapala, be it the Original Floating model, the Countdown Sinking model, Jointed model, Magnum Heavy Duty or Deep-Diver model, in either fresh or salt water:

1. *Always use the lightest possible rigging so as not to impede the natural swimming action of the lure.* Because of its

natural balance, buoyancy and authenticity of action, the Rapala should always be allowed to move as freely as possible. If you *must* use some terminal hardware (a wire or shock leader for saltwater, etc.), make your final connection with a *loop*, either snap or knot, that will permit free, unfettered swimming.

The reason is to permit the lure to track properly, particularly during *fast retrieve*, without spinning, tumbling or yawing. Saltwater fish, especially, are often only idly curious about a lure swimming at a slow rate of speed but are strongly attracted to a fast-moving, *naturally swimming* bait.

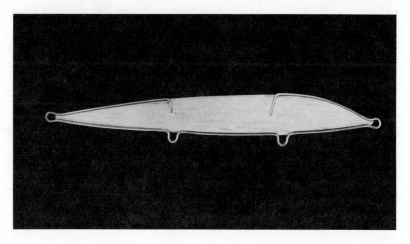

2. *Allow the built-in action of the Rapala to lure the fish into striking.* As I have stated, years of painstaking work went into the design of the Rapala Lures. This subtle swimming action for most fishing conditions will be the most productive action you can impart to the lure. We have stated that heavy rigging, lines, leaders, etc., should not be used to impede this natural swimming action. The same is true for persistent jerking, twitching, pumping or erratically changing the action of the Rapala Lures. Allow them to swim in their most natural manner for most fishing conditions. This is not to say that speed cannot be varied as the Rapala is so well balanced that it can be retrieved extremely slowly to

an entire range of speeds, including speed trolling at velocities of 5 to 6 miles per hour. However, for most fishing applications, a normal rate of retrieve imparting a lifelike action to the lure will produce the most fish.

A final word on imitations: While hundreds of lures might purport to *look* like the Rapala, none has achieved its uniquely, realistic action. The reason is that none of the imitators is made with the same fine attention to detail, the handcrafting, the balancing and adjusting that goes into each individual Rapala without fail.

No imitator has learned the secret of Lauri Rapala or has taken the time to give you the fish-catching action of his lures. Certainly, some of the other look-alikes might catch fish, but none will catch fish under all conditions like the Rapala.

I have carefully read and approved all of the following stories in this book. Most were written by my friends and fishing buddies; some of the most successful anglers in the far-flung fraternity of sportfishing. I can vouch for their insights into the best ways of using our lures. I guarantee that if you follow their suggestions you will greatly improve your own skills and stringers. We share these secrets with you because we truly appreciate your patronage and are sure that the Rapala will continue to increase your fishing pleasure!

BILL CULLERTON

A grandson of one of the 47 founders of the Izaak Walton League and a teen-age professional fly-tier for that esteemed progenitor, "Smiling Bill" Jamison, Bill Cullerton has been fishing ever since he could walk. Now, as a leading "outdoorsman," and producer (as well as the star!) of more than 30 angling films, Bill travels in Seven League Boots, skipping all over the globe to master all forms of sportfishing.

Bill, a member of the Fresh Water Fishing Hall of Fame, has been active in the American fishing tackle industry for more than 30 years. During that time, he has become angling's most serious student of knots. He makes the telling point that although a knot might appear insignificant, it may be the determining factor between landing and losing a trophy fish. Whenever he meets a new fisherman, Bill always asks for two things: to hear his favorite shark story and to see his favorite knot. From that interest in all aspects of knotmaking has come the following story. It is by far the best your editors have ever seen. Read it and we're sure that you will agree.

WHY KNOT?

It happened like it does in the dozens of articles you've read in various magazines on tarpon fishing. Tom and I were floating quietly down the Parismina River. I was proud of the near-perfect cast I had placed next to the river bank. My Rapala had travelled barely a few feet when it stopped. From the dark depths of this brooding Costa Rican river came this silver torpedo exploding the surface water into a million fragmented diamond drops.

"Tarpon!" I cried. I wanted to make sure that Tom and our guide noticed the strike; after all, it had been a slow day. The fish reached the pinnacle of his leap and seemed to hang there, motionless, for an instant. I swear I thought he had looked me right in the eye, maybe had smiled a bit, though this would have been difficult since he had the big Rapala tightly clenched in his jaws. Then the tarpon turned on his afterburner and plunged back into the river. Suddenly, the fish seemed to be everywhere at once.

I reacted quickly (though Tom said it was at least 30 seconds later) by reeling furiously to take up the slack. There was a limpness now, as the walnut size knot I had used to tie the shock leader (100 lb. test mono) to the casting line hit the tip top of my rod and wouldn't fit through. At the end of the leader was the funniest curly-cue you have ever seen. I remember swearing that that tarpon must have had paws and somehow slipped the knot apart, as I was positive that I had tied the knot properly.

By now Tom, who had seen me blow more tarpon in a few days than a man is entitled to in a lifetime, decided that he should help me. My "string" had run out, so to speak, as I had gone through every knot I knew, including the "Figure 8" and the one I had used on my "tennies."

For the next few evenings it was knots, knots, and more

13

knots. I found out that the "Bimini Twist" is not a native dance and that you don't need an M.D. to tie a Surgeon's Knot.

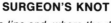

SURGEON'S KNOT

For tying a leader to a line end, where the diameters are unequal.

1. Overlap ends of lines for several inches. Tie a simple overhand knot treating both strands as one.

2. Pass the two strands through the loop again. Pull up tight. Trim ends. For greater strength, tie a "Double Surgeon's Knot" by passing the strands through the loop four times.

That Costa Rican trip and knot-tying session occurred a long time ago; since then knots have become a kind of hobby with me. You can use the very best rods, reels and lines, but if those knots are not tied properly, a big fish will have no difficulty securing his freedom. It seems ironic that sportsmen will travel to very expensive fishing lodges, buy the best gear, hire the most knowledgeable guides, only to blow that trophy fish simply because of an inefficient knot.

I've collected the following information on knots from many expert fishermen who took the time and patience to share their knowledge with me. The first thing I discovered is that very few knots are original; either a Greek fisherman used the knot 2,000 years ago, or an angler's brother-in-law has been tying the knot for years. So with apologies to inventors or originators of knots, I will identify them by their popular names.

I found out other things, too. Just because a knot is extremely difficult or complicated to tie doesn't mean it is the best knot (tougher is not always better). Also, knots can affect the action of a lure; in fact, some knots can actually "kill" the action. Finally, I have been working sport shows for more than 25 years; most of the people I talk to seem to be good casters, can retrieve a lure with pizzazz, and can fight fish effectively. But very few of these fishermen are experienced in, or confident at, tying knots.

Obviously, it will be impossible to "detail" all fishing knots, so I'll attempt to describe and recommend knots that will complement the Rapala.

Let's discuss the various uses of the knots illustrated here. For most of my Rapala fishing, I like to use a combination of the Palomar and Spider-Hitch Knots. I should explain that I almost always use a shock leader even in ultra-light fishing. Let's say I'm using 4 lb. test line. In most cases I'll probably use a few feet of 8 lb. test mono as a leader. First, I'll double four, five, or more feet of the running line (in this case, the 4 lb. test) by using the Spider-Hitch Knot described below. Another knot, the Bimini Twist is

---

SPIDER HITCH

Creates a double line with the full strength of unknotted mono. Much easier to tie than the Binimi Twist.

1. Double-up length of line desired and form a loop. Hold loop between thumb and forefinger with thumb slightly extended past finger.

2. Wrap doubled line five or more times around thumb and loop so that wraps line evenly and parallel on your thumbnail.

3. Pass end of doubled line through loop and slowly draw wraps one at a time off thumb. Pull ends and doubled line alternately to tighten. Clip off excess.

PALOMAR KNOT

A basic knot for tying on hooks, lures, swivels, etc. You may find it easier to tie than the Improved Clinch Knot. Properly tied it's just as strong.

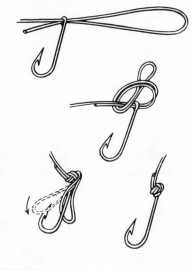

1. Pass line through eye of hook and return through eye making a 3" or 4" loop as shown.

2. Hold line and hook eye with one hand and use other hand to tie a loose overhand knot in doubled line. Do not tighten.

3. Hold loose overhand knot and pull loop over hook, swivel or lure.

4. Pull on doubled line to draw knot up making sure loop does not hang up in hook eye or swivel. Pull both line ends to tighten. Clip off end about ⅛" from knot.

slightly stronger, but much more complicated to tie. I can attach the double line (4 lb. test) to about four or five feet of 8 lb. mono (the shock leader) by using the Surgeon's Knot. The lure then can be tied to the Rapala lure using the very efficient Palomar Knot.

There are several advantages to the above rigging and knots. First, they will slide through the rod guides with ease. Secondly, the shock leader will withstand any abrasion against rocks, and as we all know, many species of fish during a fight will often run the lure and leader against rocks in order to get rid of the plug. But most importantly, you can pressure the fish more efficiently toward the end of the fight and land it quickly, since the double line will already be partially in your reel, and thus, you can apply almost eight pounds (theoretically) of pressure instead of four.

The Uni-Knot, which has gained a good deal of fame recently, is one I often use with the floating Rapalas. These top-water plugs fish much better with a loop knot.

BIMINI TWIST

This is used to make a loop or double line without excessively reducing the breaking strength of the line.

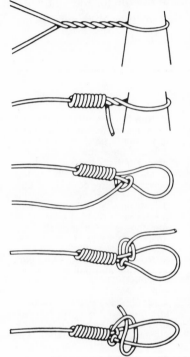

1. Double the end of the line forming a loop allowing extra line to work with. Put the loop around some stable object like a cleat or rod butt to keep the loop open. While keeping the line taut, make 20 tight twists in the lines.

2. Holding the twists tight, wind the end of the line over the twist until you reach the neck of the loop; keep these wraps tight and compact.

3. Make a half-hitch around one side of the loop; pull it tight.

4. Make another half-hitch around the other side of the loop; pull it tight.

5. To complete the Bimini Twist, make 3 half-hitches around the base of the loop, tighten it and clip off the excess line at the end.

If you want a stronger and smoother knot between the leader and doubled running line, use the Stu Apte Improved Blood Knot instead of the Surgeon's Knot. It takes just a little longer and might seem more complicated, but once you get the hang of it, it is easy to tie. Nearly everyone knows the Improved Clinch Knot, which is far superior to the normal Clinch Knot.

For some saltwater fishing, like tarpon, you will have to use a much heavier mono for a shock leader, since this fish's jaws will generally make short work of anything less than 60 lb. mono. Most tarpon men use 80 lb. or even 100 lb. test mono. The lure can be attached with either the Improved Clinch Knot or the Homer

Rhode Loop Knot, which many anglers prefer. This knot is great for a heavy leader, but it is basically a weak knot and should be avoided with the lighter lines.

When pulling a knot tight, be sure to moisten the knot with some saliva. The saliva will lubricate the mono, and you will get a much tighter knot. Remember that a knot that slips generally breaks (with the exception of the Uni-Knot).

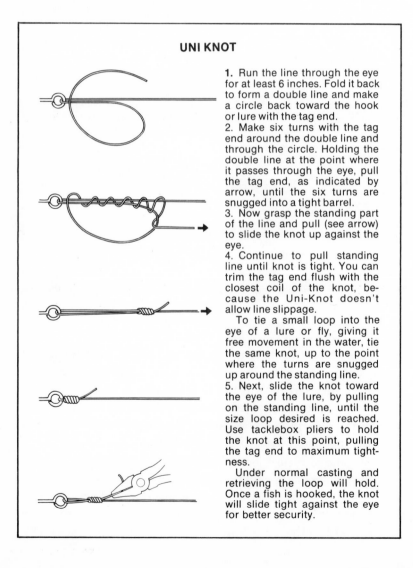

UNI KNOT

1. Run the line through the eye for at least 6 inches. Fold it back to form a double line and make a circle back toward the hook or lure with the tag end.

2. Make six turns with the tag end around the double line and through the circle. Holding the double line at the point where it passes through the eye, pull the tag end, as indicated by arrow, until the six turns are snugged into a tight barrel.

3. Now grasp the standing part of the line and pull (see arrow) to slide the knot up against the eye.

4. Continue to pull standing line until knot is tight. You can trim the tag end flush with the closest coil of the knot, because the Uni-Knot doesn't allow line slippage.

To tie a small loop into the eye of a lure or fly, giving it free movement in the water, tie the same knot, up to the point where the turns are snugged up around the standing line.

5. Next, slide the knot toward the eye of the lure, by pulling on the standing line, until the size loop desired is reached. Use tacklebox pliers to hold the knot at this point, pulling the tag end to maximum tightness.

Under normal casting and retrieving the loop will hold. Once a fish is hooked, the knot will slide tight against the eye for better security.

BLOOD KNOT

The best knot we know for tying line to line when the diameters of the two are the same or nearly so. Makes a strong, small joint that slips through most rod guides easily.

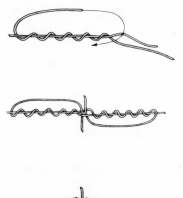

1. Overlap the ends of the two lines for several inches. Hold at the middle of the overlap and twist one end around the other line five or more turns. Bring end back and through strands as shown.

2. Still holding the lines, turn other end around line the same number of turns in the opposite direction. Bring end back and pass between lines from opposite direction of first end.

3. Tighten by pulling up slowly on both lines. Clip off ends short, or tie the knot with one end long, to use as a dropper for two-hook fishing.

STU APTE IMPROVED BLOOD KNOT

For tying a much heavier diameter line to thinner.

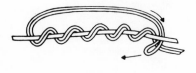

1. Double up the thinner line. Tie the same way as the Blood Knot treating doubled line as one.

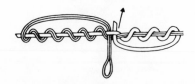

2. Use five twists of doubled up thin line, but only three turns of the heavier line.

Use a nail clipper to trim all knots. If you have pulled up your knot properly and tight, you need not be afraid of trimming it very close. When trimming mono, I always clip the ends at a 45 degree angle to the main line. This begins a taper that helps the knot slide through the guides.

Here's another tip that will help bigger knots pass through the guides more smoothly. Coat the knot with any good air-drying, waterproof glue, such as Pliobond®. It is time consuming and takes some effort, but it is these "little things" that can mean the difference between success and failure just as you are about to land that trophy fish of a lifetime.

Experts like Stu Apte, "Lefty" Kreh, and others will tie a knot, check it, and test it. If it does not look right, they will break it and start from scratch. This is why these fishermen continually land the bigger fish and claim world records.

Think about it another way. An improperly tied knot can weaken a line by as much as 50%. This means if you are using a 4 lb. test line, it could be weakened to 2 lbs. The consistent trophy-takers have everything in their favor. If they are using a 4 lb. test line, by God, it will test very close to that, even the knots. Take the time to learn these knots. Try them before you go fishing, so that you can practically tie them with your eyes shut. I'll guarantee that you will bring in bigger fish and tell fewer stories "about the ones that got away."

Illustrations courtesy of Dupont® Corporation

BUCK PERRY

*No anthology on sportfishing could claim the name without the
inclusion of a key chapter by Buck Perry. Many will tell you (and
the editors of this book agree) that Buck single-handedly invented,
discovered, staked-out and gave a formal organization to the
most comprehensive and systematic body of knowledge of how and
why game fish behave as they do.*

*The gentle North Carolinian would probably disclaim some of
those categorial statements. But they are true, all of them. And
Buck, at long last, is gaining some of the fame that has been his
due for so long. The "Father of Structure Fishing," the man who
gave us the such precise terms as "sanctuary", "scatterpoint" and
"migration route" is now Education Editor of FISHING FACTS
magazine, a publication which has done yoeman work in educating
anglers. Buck also writes books about fishing and offers courses
on his now-standard methods of angling.*

*As the following story demonstrates, Buck Perry has a rare knack
for helping his students (and that includes even the most experienced fishermen) see for themselves the beauty and elegance of
his system. Read it. Then read it again. There is much to be
gained by us all.*

BUCK TALKS ABOUT BASICS

When speaking to a group of fishermen, a slide projector is often used to screen a picture of a natural or man-made lake. The question is asked, "How many of you can tell me where the fish are in this lake? Sometime I will get an answer such as, "In the water", but most of the time they just sit there in complete silence. Then it is pointed out that *the fish are either in the shallows, the deep, or someplace between.* This statement usually takes a little time to sink in, but without fail it produces a lot of laughs.

After the laughter subsides, my next comment is normally, "What are you laughing about? That observation wasn't meant to be a funny, it was made to point out a *basic fishing fact.* And, you had better keep it in mind if you desire to catch fish consistently in the future."

When talking about the proper presentation of lures, it is pointed out that fishing gear must be looked upon as "tools". These "tools" *must allow you to accomplish the things you are trying to do at a particular time and place.* If the gear you use will not allow you to do the things you are trying to do, they are not the right tools, and should not be used. Then, another basic fishing fact is pointed out—"In order to catch a fish, you must be at the right place, at the right time, fishing in the right manner. If *any* of these things are off, you will not catch a fish".

When discussing mapping and interpretation of a body of water, it is pointed out that a lot can be accomplished by a study of the terrain, looking at the color of the water, talking to other fishermen, locating all the "hot spots", obtaining and studying a contour map, looking the areas over with a depth sounder, etc. BUT, in the final analysis, the only way a complete interpretation can be made about the lake, or a particular "structure", *is to put lures down there and find out – by catching a fish.* If you catch a fish you are at the right place at the right time, fishing in the right manner. However, if your lures will not allow you to fish in the right manner at any particular time and place, you will not get an interpretation of the lake (or structure), nor will you catch a fish. Most of you will agree that our "lures" must not only allow us to "fish" them at the right place, but they must also produce the desired reaction from the fish. In other words, if we can place them correctly we should get a "take".

FIGURE 1

To be sure we understand what is meant by fishing correctly at the right place and time, let's look at a drawing. Figure 1 is a side view of a fishing situation you and I will experience quite often. You will note the fish are located in an "in between" position. They are not in the shallowest water, nor are they in the deepest water. Let's assume you are the person fishing the area, and you are using your favorite surface lure. The question is, are you fishing in the right place, at the right time, in the correct manner? You will probably arrive at the same conclusion I do: Your "time" may be correct, but how about the right place and the manner of presentation?

I believe you will agree that our lures must allow us to *CONTROL* our presentation. If we desire to put them at a particular place, move them a certain way, have them "look" right to the fish; then, our selection of lures must be made other than looking for something pretty, something we prefer, or something we have heard has caught a fish. With this thought in mind, let's consider some of the things we might "control". This should then give us some sort of guide as to what we should have in our tackle box.

You and I can't control the weather, the water conditions, nor the appetite of the fish. We can't control the amount of traffic on the water, the reproduction of the fish, the temperature, the amount of oxygen in the water or its color. We can't do much about how deep the lake is (or the fish), nor how dirty or clean the bottom. We have little to say about the type or degree of "structure". Things of this nature vary by the thousands, and probably we would never run into the exact conditions any two times in our fishing career.

At first you might think there is little we can control. After a little thought you might think there are lots of things we can control. But, after a great deal of thought, you will probably arrive at the same conclusion I did. The things that we can actually *control* in the presentation of lures are DEPTH, SPEED, SIZE, COLOR and ACTION. It is likely you thought of other controls, but you probably asked yourself, "Is it possible to control them? Will it do any good? Do I have time to check it out? How will I know if it's good or bad?"

Let's look at these controls and see if they will help us in the selection of the "tools" (lures, in this case) we should be using at any particular time and place. The first thing that glares is the fact that there are FIVE things. This could represent such a multitude of combinations we couldn't hope to try them all in a season of fishing, much less on any particular fishing trip. Therefore we had better look at these things very closely and see if we can't reduce their number, or do something to improve our chances of being at the right place at the right time, fishing in the right manner on a particular fishing trip.

ACTION CONTROL

Most manufacturers have built ACTION into their lures. Some have done a better job than others. A few will give enough thought and time to the design so as to produce a "take" or a "strike" if the lure is presented properly to the fish. To my way of thinking, Rapala has done just that.

There is little you and I can do about this "Action" and as fishermen we should not be too concerned about it (provided the manufacturer has done a good job). *We should view this control more as adjunct to "Speed" control.* If we consider it as a distinct and separate control, we are putting our faith in a particular wiggle of the lure, *over which we have no control.* We should view "Action" more as an AID in catching fish, rather than an absolute control. Every available action could be used, but if it wasn't used at the right place at the right time (depth control), and moved so as produce a "take" (speed control) it would not put fish on the stringer. What good would the fine action built into the Rapala be, if you did not put it where the fish are (depth control) and did not move it at the right speed? Would you get action without speed control (how fast you moved the lure)?

COLOR CONTROL

At times the fish *do* appear to have a color preference. At times certain water conditions tend to make certain colors more attractive to fish. But we should see that existing light conditions probably govern any color preference. But, here again we have a multitude of variables. Not only will the light vary from day to day, but from hour to hour. What do we do? Do we go through our lures looking for one particular color the fish might hit?

Too often, too much emphasis is placed on color. If a fisherman had a color that would prove to be the most delectable morsel a fish could desire, and he fished it around a bush, or weedbed, in the shoreline shallows and the fish were at 25 feet, the fish wouldn't be likely to know that delicious tidbit was available. Again, if that "magic" color wasn't moved (speed control) to show the fish it was around, what good would it do?

We should look at color in the proper perspective. It can be *"controlled"* by a simple hand rule. *If conditions are bright (clear day, clear water, etc.) use bright lures. If conditions are dark (cloudy, early or late, dingy water, etc.) use darker lures.* This type of color control will put it more in the form of an AID rather than an absolute control. Testing to see if one color is preferable to another presents no problem. The hand rule will eliminate color as a concern or worry. AND, *this rule of thumb will suffice to locate the fish.* After all, we can't say a particular color is preferable until we have located the fish. Once they are located we can test to see if one color is better than another. With this type of color control in mind, we can never go wrong in having more than one color in our tackle box. The Rapala people have made available the colors that may be preferable under the many light conditions that you and I face.

SIZE CONTROL

Many fishermen stick with one particular size, or weight, lure regardless of the time and the place they are fishing. They give no thought that there might be a size preference as far as the fish is concerned, or THAT HE (the fisherman) MAY GET BETTER DEPTH AND SPEED CONTROL, IF THE LURE SIZE OR WEIGHT WERE CHANGED.

We should never look at a lure size in respect to the size of fish we are trying to catch. A good rule of thumb to keep in mind is: A game fish will try to eat anything as big as he is, and will often take a shot at something bigger. A lure size-preference may exist under certain circumstances and with some species. In some colder waters a smaller lure may be more desirable than a larger lure. But, as the water warms and the metabolism of the fish increases, a larger lure may be more attractive than a smaller lure.

You and I should set up another rule of thumb if we are to approach size (control) in an intelligent manner. Lure size (and weight) is important from the standpoint of getting better control in our presentation. You should see that if we wanted to work a particular depth, we would have to use a lure size and weight that would allow us to move it in such a way to get the action (speed control) YET ALLOW US TO MAINTAIN THE DEPTH. If we lost our depth (where the fish are) when we tried to get the right action (speed control) we are in trouble.

Better control can be had with larger or heavier lures as we go deeper. Also, we are likely to have better size control as far as any preference is concerned. The food of the fish is normally stacked that way, and certainly the fish can see the lure better. Most of the time the larger fish are deeper than the smaller fish, and most large fish prefer a "mouthful" as he is probably no longer able (or desires) to run all over the place picking up a little dab here and a little dab there.

To put size in its proper perspective *we should at all times use size and weights that will allow us to present lures correctly for the time and place.* Rapala has come up with the sizes and weights and designs which will allow us to do most of the things we will be called upon to do. We can't expect one particular lure to do all the work that may be required to put the fish on the stringer in different fishing situations.

At this stage, we have not completely eliminated any of the five original Controls, but we have reduced three of them (Size, Color, Action) to a catagory of AIDS rather than absolute controls. We have reduced the multitude of possible combinations down to just a few. It doesn't mean we are completely "out of the woods", but it does mean you and I are not faced with things we can't do something about in a reasonable length of time. It's at this point that we must look upon our lures more in the term of TOOLS, and our whole consideration is to put them at the right place at the right time, and in the right manner.

SPEED CONTROL

When considering the control of how fast we move the lures, you might think a better word could have been used. You might say we should have used the word "velocity" instead of the word "speed". You might say some fishermen will get the idea that the word "speed" means "fast". This is one of the reasons the word "speed" was used instead of the more correct word "velocity". The average fisherman has never been concerned with how fast his lure moves through the water. He has been plagued through the years with misinformation about how "slow" a lure must be worked, and that any thought of using a faster speed was out of the question. The word "speed" was used to *impress* upon the fishermen the importance of *controlling* the velocity with which the lure moves through the water. It does not necessarily mean that the velocity is always fast. If we work a lure in such a way as to let it remain still for a moment, without any movement, then the "speed" is zero. Speed can vary from zero to very, very fast. Who is to say what speed is required with a particular lure, or a particular fish?

What are the areas and conditions affecting the speeds, or how fast we move our lures?

Air and water *temperature* are the primary conditions that will determine the speed of our lures. As the air and water temperatures go up, so does our speed. As the temperature goes down so does the speed of our lures. Shallow water and deep water have different speed requirements. Faster and more varied speeds may be called for in the shallows than when working deep water. A basic rule of thumb would be: as you get deeper and deeper, the slower and slower the speed. *However*, in either the shallows or in the deep, the best speed can only be determined at the time of fishing. The only way to determine the correct speed is to "check it out". This can be done by starting with just enough speed to produce some action in the lure. Then, at intervals, increase the speed with which the lure moves through the water. Only by varying the speed can the most productive one be found. You may be surprised at the number of times when you think the fish can't catch the lure, you are just getting close to the best speed required. You can throw all your best sizes, colors and actions along a particular shoreline, but if you have not considered SPEED control, you probably haven't "fished" the area. Because of its balance, the Rapala runs true over a wide range of lure speeds. The fisherman must "check them out".

DEPTH CONTROL

Depth Control should be looked upon as the most important control in fishing. To put depth control in its simplest form, we could say "You have to fish the shallow water, the deep water and all the depths in-between (for the purpose of getting the lure to the fish)". Many fishermen do not know or take into consideration, that fish change their depth. The depth at which a fish will be is primarily controlled by the weather and water conditions. These conditions will change throughout the year, the month, the day and the hour. These changes will, in turn, change the depth at which the fish will be found. However, you and I must approach depth control in a much broader sense that just placing lures shallow and deep. WHERE and HOW to test the water to arrive at the fish must be based on different species, different seasons, different water conditions, different weather conditions, different lakes, different structures, different bottom conditions, different time periods, etc.

I could make this list much longer, but these few should show the broad areas covered by DEPTH control. All the controls previously talked about would be of little value without a thorough understanding of this subject. This article is not the place nor the time to discuss the many aspects of depth control. Suffice it to say that you can't catch fish "where they 'ain't!". (Editors' note: Buck thoroughly covers this subject, as well as many more, in his books and his new Encyclopedia of Fishing Facts. Information on these publications can be obtained by writing Buck at P.O. Box 66   Hickory, N.C. 28601)

As we look at the controls that you and I must consider if we desire consistent success in our fishing, it becomes very obvious that we must select lures that will give us maximum control at all times. Let us look at some typical fishing situations which you and I will encounter.

FIGURE 2

Figure 2 is a side view of a typical fishing situation. The weather and water conditions have produced a condition where the fish have moved to the shallows and are located around the shallows weeds, brush, etc. Our main job is to put our lures where the fish are (depth control) and move them in such a way to make the fish take (speed control). If we do that, we are at the right place, at the right time, fishing in the right manner. This particular situation would call for lures that not only have the right size, color and action (use hand rules) but they must be designed so we encounter no problems in checking the area successfully. The original floating models of the Rapala would give excellent control in a situation such as this.

FIGURE 3

Figure 3 is another situation that you and I will encounter. In this case the weather and water conditions have the fish in deeper water. They are not going to move any shallower than the edge of the deepest weeds. It would not appear we could make contact with the fish if we used surface or shallow running lures. In order to reach the fish, we will have to use lures so designed as to run at greater depths. Whether on the cast or on the troll, we would be wise in using a lure such as the Rapala Deep-Diver series.

FIGURE 4

Figure 4 is a fishing situation you and I will face a great deal of the time. The movements of the fish from the deep water has not occurred. They are quite deep and quite inactive. That is, they are dormant and non-chasing. This means you and I must not only put the lures "right on the money", but we must be able to check the spot without pulling our lures away too fast or too far. This will call for a sinking "jump" type lure such as the Pilkki Jigging Rapala. We may have to position our boat in deep water in order to reach the fish. It is possible we may have to locate the boat directly over them and fish straight up and down.

FIGURE 5

Figure 5 is a tall weedline situation. The weedline could be as tall as 15-17 feet. The fish are at the base of the weedline. This means we should get our lures to the base of the weedline, to the bottom. You could use either the Countdown sinking Rapala, allowing it to settle to the bottom before making your retrieve, or by casting the Deep-Diver Rapala, which floats at rest, but will dive nearly vertically to these depths. It should be obvious that our best position to work the base of the weedline is to position the boat close to the weeds and make our casts parallel with them.

FIGURE 6

Figure 6 is a situation where the fisherman has checked out the shallows and the "in-between" with different style Rapalas. He has not found the fish, and has wisely gone "downstairs" looking for them. He has located them around a bush sitting on the edge of the channel. He found he had to use a sinking-type lure, but he also found if he let the lure sink too deep, such as into the bottom of the channel, he would get hung up on the edge of the channel, or on the bush before he had a chance at the fish. It didn't take him long to realize he was in a situation he had been in before where he encountered the fish around a deep weedbed. He would have to let his lure sink just so far and no deeper. With a Countdown Rapala he had the lure tipping, or ripping, "jus' rite" through the twigs in short order.

I feel that this story has told in a basic, but very *usable* way, how the full family of Rapala lures gives you the tools to exert the five Controls we use when we're fishin' "smart." That is: a systematic, educated way of using the variables found in any given angling situation; instead of letting those variables "use" us.

If there is any one thing I would like to accomplish on my travels through this wonderful world, it is to sell *EDUCATION* in fishing: to take the "by-guess and by-golly" aspects out of the sport and lead anglers to an understanding of how best to use the tools at hand for catching fish. They are, really, all we've got.

I feel that the various Rapalas are first and foremost among those tools. By studying the stories in this book and consulting my writings, particularly the new Encyclopedia of Fishing Facts, I'm sure you'll do increasingly well on the water. We're all here to help each other. Isn't that what fishing is all about?

ROLAND MARTIN

"Bassmaster" magazine recently answered its own question with the name of Roland Martin when it asked, "Who is the all-time top point champion of the national BASS Tournament Trail?" Not only is the Broken Arrow, Oklahoma, angler the all-time BASS point leader, but he also ranks as the all-time first-place winner with eight tournament victories and the leader in money winnings with $47,823.80 in earnings.

Still only in his mid-30's, Roland has already rung up an impressive array of achievements in other areas. A graduate of the University of Maryland with a degree in the biological sciences, Roland has also worked in product research and development for Lowrance Electronics, helping in the evolution of the famous Lo-K-Tor and several other scientific aids to angling.

His newest venture is the production of a syndicated TV program on the out-of-doors now going into national distribution. It's called "Fishing with Roland Martin" and its aim is to help you become a better angler: to be able to fish just like Roland. For starters, please consider the following story on catching lunker bass.

PATTERN FISHING FOR LUNKER BASS

I got turned on to the fantastic ability of the Rapala to catch really lunker bass back in 1966, during my seven years as a fishing guide on Santee Cooper, a 190,000 acre reservoir in South Carolina.

Through hard-won knowledge of that lake, I was able to formulate a *complete system of bass fishing;* one that gives the serious angler the tools to handle all types of lures in all kinds of waters to catch fish in all four seasons. It sounds all-inclusive, and it is. And I'm going to share it with you now for the first time in any publication, anywhere.

Pattern System of Bass Fishing

I call it the Pattern System of bass fishing because it involves three basic ingredients common to angling for all members of this specie. If you monitor these elements very carefully, you will find *repeating patterns of bass behavior*, no matter what season or the water you are fishing.

The three ingredients of the Pattern System of bass fishing are: 1. Cover
  2. Depth
  3. Structure

All of these terms are used in the common sense and their meanings will become apparent in what follows.

Further, the relatedness of the three basic ingredients results in three pronounced Rapala-based techniques which give us a greatly simplified approach to fishing for giant bass:

TYPE OF PATTERN	TYPE OF RAPALA
Spawning Pattern	Original Floating Rapala
Summer Pattern	Floating *and* Countdown Rapala
Lunker Pattern	Deep-Diver Rapala

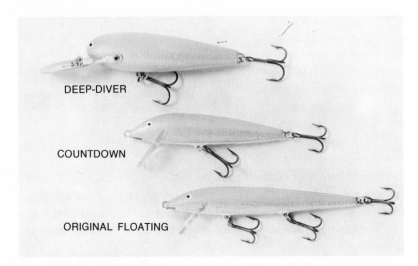

DEEP-DIVER

COUNTDOWN

ORIGINAL FLOATING

The Spawning Pattern

In my early, experimental days on Cooper Santee, I discovered that bass spawn in water temperatures of 62 to 72 degrees F., migrating into the clear, shallow back bays or "clearwater ponds" on the *full moons* of March, April or May to prepare to spawn.

When I began, it was easier to spot the big females on their

spawning beds than it was to get them to strike! I tried plastic worms, a variety of surface plugs and even live bait, but without any great degree of success.

Continuing to experiment, I found that the best method, by far, was to cast to the nesting, "hog" bass with the #11, 4⅜″ original floating Rapala on an 8 or 10 lb. test monofilament line with a conventional spinning rig.

Throw your #11 Rapala directly on top of the spawning bed. Let it lie there, motionless, for a long period of time, until all of the ripples die away. Then slowly, very slowly, twitch it out of there. If it's a really big bass, and now I'm talking about 7, 8, 9 or even 10 lb. females, it might take several casts before she hits.

When she does offer, you will discover that she will actually suck the Rapala in, much as a bluegill inhales a popper with that familiar "slurping" sound. But the similarity ends there!! If you're lucky, the bass will have completely inhaled the plug, with none of it protruding to hang up on cover. In fact, I prefer to *wade* the little black lakes of Cooper Santee while fishing the spawning pattern, chasing after hooked fish on foot, hopeful that they don't find anything deeper than the two to three feet in which they spawn!

Branching out from Santee, I continued to find identical spawning patterns in widely different parts of the country. For instance, I won my very first National Bass Tournament in Florida's Lake Seminole in 1970 on a combination of three lures. Early in the morning I caught the most, and biggest, of my largemouth on the #11, silver Rapala. Later in the day I switched to plastic worms and wound up the afternoon using spinnered, top-water plugs. All three varieties caught bass. But there is no doubt in my mind that the #11 silver Rapala is the finest bait there is for taking spawning largemouth bass in any waters, anywhere.

Here are some helpful tips for this kind of fishing: improve your line strength by *doubling* the last foot or two of your mono. (See Bill Cullerton's article on Knots in this book, for details.) I particularly like the *Bimini Twist*. With it, I find I can pursuade even the most headstrong bass to come along through the grass, brush and lily pads without shaking loose or breaking the line.

The later vegetation, by the way, is preferred spawning cover in many parts of the country, as are little "button bushes', willow snags, logs and stumps. In the TVA reservoirs of Tennessee and Kentucky, bass seems to prefer to spawn in the shallows, near the black stumps.

With a pair of polaroid glasses, I find it easy to spot the fish on her circular spawning nest near the cover. Cast directly to the bed and *let your #11 sit there at least 10 seconds, until all ripples subside.* Then twitch the Rapala. On first move, it might invoke only a defensive stance on the part of the bass. But when *moved very slowly,* she perceives it as a constant threat and is finally goaded into banishing (she thinks!) the intruder. That's when the fun begins!!

Spawning Pattern-Summation

The Spawning Pattern of bass fishing demands the following three basic requirements:

1.) Water Temperature of at least 62 degrees—a prerequisite for all surface action.
2.) Water clarity of at least two or three feet, so the nesting female can see the Rapala.
3.) Depth and Cover for spawning of less than 5 feet—because shallow water warms first and spawning fish also feel more secure with sanctuary nearby.

The Summer Pattern

As the season progresses, water temperatures rise and the bass complete their spawning, there is a transition into what I call the Summer Pattern of bass fishing. Early on in this progression, when water temperatures move into the 70's, bass begin to look for an *ambush point* from which they can feed.

Because bass don't have eyelids, *shade from the sun* is basic to any ambush point: the shelter of a dock, stump, grass, lily pads, etc. They lie in this cover, which is really a form of structure, and await the opportunity to feed.

The #11 floating Rapala is still my choice for fishing bass on the ambush point. But the casting now must be more precise because of the structure that affords cover. Any kind of wind complicates the problem to presentation. My suggestion is to

throw *upwind* of your target and let the wind slowly push your lure into proximity of the ambush point. Again, *slowly twitch* your Rapala out of there and wait for the big smash!

I find this technique super good not only in the morning and evening in the early summer (when there is often less wind) but also in the middle of the day, *as long as there is the shade of an ambush point.* Even the hot, Southern midsummer does *not* take the sizzle out of this approach. I've twitched the #11 for lots of big bass in 90 degree temperatures in 4 or 5 feet of water in Santee Cooper, Sam Rayburn and other big reservoirs, but always out of the direct sunlight, usually in the morning or evening.

Of course, the #11 floater is also a good fall and early winter lure, I consider surface plugs to be effective until the water temperature slips below 60 degrees. In the 60-70 degree range, I fish the #11 all day, ideally under overcast skies, but always in the shade in the event of sunlight. The basic Rapala even takes Florida bass in January and February, if I can find water of the correct temperature.

In Florida, however, the other slow, brackish, backup waters of the Southern tidal areas, I lean toward the *gold colored* #11. The golden shiner is the main forage fish of bass in these waters and the 11G seems to approximate the color of this shiner better than any other lure.

The Summer Pattern - Countdown Rapala

One of the basic variables of the Pattern System of bass fishing is *water clarity.* Its presence, or absence, tells us, to a large degree, at what depths to look for bass. For example, there are many large lakes and reservoirs with relatively *clear* water, water with 8 to 10 feet of vertical visibility.

These lakes often provide little cover aside from the natural structure of rock and gravel bars, long sloping points, old creek beds, etc. The TVA reservoirs of Kentucky and Tennessee are examples of this kind of water, as are the deep glacial lakes of Canada and our North country. (Typically, many of these lakes contain large populations of *crayfish,* a bass staple particularly relished by smallmouth.)

This kind of habitat is literally designed for the sinking, Countdown Rapala series: deep, clear water with lots of geographic structure and abounding with crayfish. When fishing this kind of water, I automatically reach for a #9 or #11 Countdown Rapala, either silver or gold in color; depending on water coloration, the natural food chain and other local conditions. Again, I prefer a regular spinning outfit, tying the 8 or 10 pound test monofilament line directly to this gently sinking lure. There is even less risk of hangup here than in fishing the spawning beds or ambush points.

On waters like these, I find a good electronic locator and an accurate contour map of great value in finding pronounced structure in depths of from 15 to 30 feet off the shoreline. It is in such spots—atop well-defined bars, along sloping underwater points or in old creek channels, etc.—that you expect to find schooling bass, up to 20 or 30 in a group, including many large fish.

The aim, of course, is to find the *depth* of the bass. They might be at almost any level above the thermocline, in water temperatures between 52 and 80 degrees, although they seem to prefer temperatures between 60 and 75, if light and other conditions permit them to hold within that range. It always helps to ask guides, the boat dock operator or knowledgeable local fishermen about the depth at which the bass might be found.

After getting on some likely structure, I use the Countdown Rapala itself to find the most productive depth; making a series of casts outward, from shallow to deeper water, allowing the lure to sink until slack line indicates that it's touching bottom, then retrieving the lure ever so slowly with the rod pointed straight at the lure.

This way, you literally bump the Countdown over, around and through any fish-holding structure, sometimes stopping and starting the lure, but *always ready for the strike, which usually comes upon picking up the slack line after a brief pause in the retrieve*. After any strike, I either drop the anchor or a marker. If I've encountered a school of smallmouth, which could be in 30 or so feet of water, I let the Countdown sink all the way to the bottom, then retrieve it in little "spurts" — reeling rapidly for a second or two, letting it sink to the bottom again. More often than not, a bass will strike on the "downstroke" — as it settles again after a little spurt.

It's also possible to slowly troll a Countdown Rapala in "prospecting" for bass and their depth. But the disadvantage is that you spend 90 percent of your time in unproductive water. It's much better to use a locator, contour map and local reports on schooling fish and their depth. Then go to work with your Countdown, either #9 or #11 in the appropriate color: silver in "clean" water, gold in habitat stained by tannins and organic material. Let the Countdown do the rest. It helps you find all kinds of big bass, and then it helps you catch 'em.

Summer Pattern—Summation

In the Summer Pattern of Bass Fishing, two kinds of Rapalas are used:

1.) The #11 original Floating model - in water temperatures from 75 to 95 degrees, at *ambush points*, with plenty of cover nearby, with the lure *twitched away*, as for spawning bass.

2.) The #9 and #11 sinking Countdown Rapalas - in clear, deeper water (below 8 feet) and retrieved slowly through the depth in which the bass are schooling, that depth determined by water temperature, clarity, structure and the other variables of the system.

The "Lunker" Pattern

If it's trophy bass you're really after, there is a brief period of the year when you might connect with one or more of those mind-boggling bass that stops all conversation. Your chances are most likely to occur in the *pre-spawning season, when water temperatures are moving up from approximately 47 degrees to the 60 degrees which put the big females on the spawning beds.*

The pre-spawning pattern finds the bass moving out of the deep water, up and along the points which lead to nesting areas. It's at this juncture that the Rapala Deep-Diver, # 70 or # 90, is, hands down, your best bet for hanging that once-in-a-lifetime bass.

I've found that what I call the *"main link points"*, the bars that jut out into the main lake a long ways from the sheltered spawning areas, are the best structure to fish for giant, pre-spawning bass. As they move up the link points, the big females seem especially pugnacious; ready to strike any intruding object more out of heedless instinct, or reflex action, than at any other time. Pre-spawning bass are in a very "catchable" mood!

Like a post-spawning bass, fish in the lunker pattern will seek out an *ambush point;* a spot behind a rock, near a stump or some other kind of cover from which it has protection from the sun and water movements caused by wind and currents that might be sweeping across the point. When you find such conditions, keep laying that Deep-Diver in there, bouncing it past the lair. Eventually the bass will hit, viciously, out of reflex action, you'll know when it's on!

As you fish such a point, take into consideration both the sun and the current. Have your plug come at the bass from the *shady* side of his ambush point, so he doesn't have to look into the sun's rays to see it. Current is also often troublesome in the Spring of the year; high waters compounded by winds that get up to 15, 20 miles an hour. *Bass will point or face into the wind every time.* They must hold, like trout, because they cannot swim backwards.

It is a *must,* then, to retrieve your Deep-Diver *with* the current, *down* wind, which means that you will have to cast *up,* or at least *across the wind.* So it's hard work. You are often casting into the teeth of a gale! Pre-spawning, lunker bass keep their heads upstream and into the wind. It's the only posture from which they will make a reflex action strike.

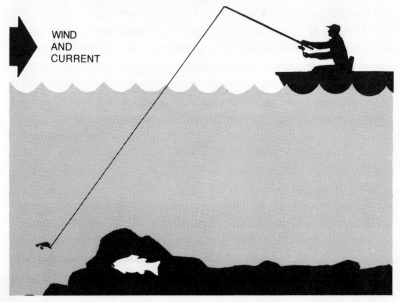

WIND
AND
CURRENT

You must fish your Deep-Diver fast. Make a lot of casts, retrieving quickly, saturating each likely area with your coverage.

It's just Bang! Bang! Bang! Hit every possible stick-up, every stump, every log, every rock. Hundreds and hundreds of casts, made quickly and accurately! Your mind is functioning like a computer: shady side, wind, sun, current, cover, ambush point! It's fishing with a controlled frenzy, making as many and as accurate casts as you can. If you can fit this pattern of fishing to lunker pattern of pre-spawning behavior, you'll have a better than average chance of coming up with that monster bass.

Summary

What I've been saying, in case you missed it, is that *pattern is everything:* pattern consisting of a certain *combination* of circumstances or conditions, such as water temperature, clarity, structure or whatever, which attract bass (or any other species) to a certain spot at a certain time.

Once I catch a bass, I check the exact depth, the exact structure and the exact cover, then immediately look for another spot identical to the first. Early in the spring, you'll find well-defined, consistent patterns of lunker bass. When you find them, the Deep-Diver Rapala is the lure to bring them up.

Thanks in large part to this lure, I have won eight major National Bass Tournaments. You can have the success by putting to work this Pattern System of Bass Fishing.

And wherever and whenever you fish for bass, you'll find a type, color and size of Rapala to fit your needs. I know, because I carry more of them in my tacklebox than any other lure!

AL LINDNER

Al cut his eye teeth on a fishing rod as a guide ... and knocked around the country as a "fishing bum" learning "what it was all about" from the bottom up. The beard is as real as he is ... the patched levis and battered moccasins aren't a costume ... They're part of his every day dress. He eats, sleeps and lives fishing. Al made fishing headlines when he was only 16 .. and continued to become a three time World Champion. In 1965 he won the Wisconsin Musky Championship .. in 1968 grabbed the World National Open Championship and won first place in the coveted $22,000 1974 Tennessee Invitational BASS Tournament. He has been the only man to win the two major walleye tournaments back to back and has participated in two Bassmaster Classics ... Al is widely acclaimed by many authorities as America's best all around fresh water fisherman. Al has been a Field Editor, for Fishing Facts and many other magazines and was featured in articles by Sports Afield, Field and Stream, Outdoor Life. Today Al does a radio show, and has hosted a syndicated outdoors T.V. show and is currently Director of the IN'FISHERMAN Society.

FISHING FOR WALLEYES
AND NORTHERN PIKE

For many years, the Rapala has been one of the most effective lures on the tackle market because it comes closest to simulating the natural forage of most game fish. Its minnowlike appearance and action makes it a very convincing bait for walleye, northern pike, lake trout, bass and muskellunge.

The types of Rapalas available—the original floater, the Countdown sinking model and the Magnum to list a few—has multiplied its applications. It can be retrieved just under the water's surface, worked slowly over the bottom, or consistantly kept at specific depths for "suspended" fish. By using different models, adjusting the speed of retrieve and amount of weight used, an angler can obtain a wide range of depths and cover them most efficiently.

Rapalas are designed for use with all types of tackle. I personally prefer spinning gear. I like a fairly stiff, six-to-seven-foot rod for trolling and casting. A high degree of "feel" is not required with Rapalas because fish usually are "automatically" hooked when they strike.

A monofilament line with little stretch—from 8-to 12-pound-test—is ideal. If you go to lighter line, you are likely to lose fish, especially when trolling. On the other hand, very heavy line will considerably impede the lifelike action of the lure.

Basically, I rig the Rapala three ways for most fishing situations. When fishing very shallow bars with a floating Rapala or the Countdown model designed to sink at a constant rate, the line should be tied with a Loop Knot directly to the lure, or use a very small snap so you won't hamper the lure's action too much. Heavy terminal tackle is taboo and will impair the action.

The best method, however, is to use a loop knot, such as a Uni-Knot. Which allows the lure to run with peak action. Leaders and large snap swivels tend to dampen the action, especially at high speeds.

Another method uses a sinker to enable a floating Rapala to reach the proper depth. Again, the lure is tied directly to the line with the loop knot. A split-shot sinker is attached to the line. The weight of the sinker depends upon the depth you want to fish and your speed. Larger floating Rapalas require more weight.

The sinker should be attached anywhere fron 24 to 36 inches in front of the lure. And, use only as much weight as you need.

This set-up works well for both casting and trolling. When trolling, adjusting the speed and the amount of line out will run the Rapala near the bottom in deep water or allow it to swim at mid-depths for suspended fish.

The other method I use employs a three-way swivel and bell sinker. I believe the Rapala can be fished much better this way because even a heavier weight does not hamper the action as much as a weight placed directly on the fishing line. One to two feet of line should separate the bell-sinker from the swivel. The length of this dropline should be changed to adapt to changing bottom conditions. A weedy or mossy bottom will require a longer dropline than a clean, sandy bottom. A shorter line also is better when fishing boulders and rocky sites. The length of line between the swivel and Rapala could range up to four feet. This length permits the floating Rapala to swim up from off the bottom. The longer length permits better lure action and the weight is not as apt to spook fish.

This set-up also is well suited to bottom-bumping techniques which often are effective. Whenever fishing a river with a swift current, this usually is the only way to fish the Rapala properly.

Now let's discuss methods for taking walleyes.

In spring, lake walleyes generally can be found quite shallow. The male fish are often in depths of only three to four feet. These holding sites are adjacent to the spawning grounds. By opening day, female walleyes tend to run somewhat deeper. Of course, the depth at which you find them will vary depending on your location, prevailing conditions and many other factors.

As a general rule, I like to start shallow when searching for walleyes in spring. This can be accomplished by systematically eliminating unproductive water quickly. In other words, trolling.

The Rapala should be rigged with the split-shot or sinkers for weight. A ¼ oz. weight us usually enough for depths of less than 12 feet. The size of the Rapala is your choice. I prefer the smaller models in spring such as the No. 9 or No. 11.

The length of line you use is vital for proper depth control. When trolling the shallows, considerable distance should be the rule, especially in clear water to avoid spooking fish. And, the farther the lure is from the boat, the deeper it will run. About 50 feet of line should keep the lure running deep enough. Depending on trolling speed, a depth between five and 10 feet can be achieved. It is best to start out rather slow, just above idle speed, and maintain a steady pace. During the cold water periods, a slow speed is usually the most effective. But you should experiment some until you discover the most productive speed.

You can troll forward quite easily with three men in a boat. But each angler should carefully watch the amount of line in the water. If all are of equal distance, there will be little problem with tangled lines.

When working bars, make an effort to maintain a constant depth throughout your trolling run to thoroughly cover that level. A depth locator is an invaluable aid in doing this. If fish contact is not made, deeper runs should be made. When you do find fish, mark the site and retroll it. If there seems to be a concentration of fish in one small area, it often is a good idea to come back and cast to the area from a distance. Too much trolling could eventually spook the school, especially in shallow, clear water.

Most walleye fishing is done near the bottom, but in summer you can sometimes take suspended fish by trolling Rapalas. If you can locate schools of bait fish running at a certain depth, adjust your lure to run slightly deeper. The walleyes will be below the bait fish, gorging themselves on the forage fish, especially ciscoes. Unless you run into them by accident, however, the only way to find them is with a locator or graph unit. The most difficult part, however, is get the lure to run at the precise depth. With this type of fishing, precise line and boat control are essential.

Each trolling run should be carefully considered so the lure will be in the "fish zone" as much as possible.

Larger Rapalas are more effective in summer. A No. 18 is very good, especially an big walleyes. The split-shot or rubber-core sinker rig is usually best in this case. The trolling speed and amount of line used should be carefully monitored to achieve maximum control. You always should be aware of how deep your lure is running. Taking suspended walleyes like this is challenging and requires plenty of practice to master. An indepth study of this angling phenomenon was included in one of our IN' FISHER-MAN Study Reports...

If you begin catching smaller male fish, move slightly deeper. You may contact the larger, females. At this time of year, males and females usually will be in the same area. The same hot spots— little "fingers," knolls and points—are used by both but at different depths.

In summer, walleye patterns change and the fishing gets tougher because the fish will hold much deeper. In certain lakes, walleyes will suspend up to 15 feet off the bottom and location becomes more difficult. But once fish are found, they usually will be tightly schooled.

Of course, the shallows will hold some scattered stray fish, particularly at night. Some good areas to fish will be near big reefs and points. Sunken islands and little rocky knobs are other excellent places.

It has been proven that the Rapala is a most effective lure at night, especially during the so-called "dog days" in July and August. On certain heavily pressured lakes, this can be the ticket to taking big walleyes, when other methods are not producing during the day.

The best times for this approach are usually just after sunset and before sunrise. Night fishing is easiest and usually more productive on a moonlit night. Special "moonglow" lights are available which emit a soft light perfect for fishing at such times.

Trolling at night, however, requires more preparation, if you want to be successful. You should have a good idea of the lake's bottom structure and terrain before you attempt a night fishing expedition. You should have a thorough knowledge of shallow reefs and deadheads for your own safety.

Walleyes can be taken quite shallow at night. The fish move up to feed. At night they will scatter more than during the day. This is why it is best to select large bars or reefs where a long trolling run can be made. The walleyes you run into probably will not be heavily schools but along the structure at intervals. Rock and gravel bars are the most likely structures to fish, but some walleye lakes have a softer, weedier bottom in the shallows. On these weedy lakes, Rapalas should, at first, be trolled along the deeper edges of the weeds. If no fish contact is made, shallower trolling runs should be tried, but with less weight on the lure, allowing it to run over the top of the weeds.

A slightly faster trolling pace seems to work well at night, but this, too, can vary with conditions. Very slow trolling, however, is usually the rule and most productive. The same methods previously discussed for trolling also apply here.

During the day, most walleyes will be at greater depths. The Rapala can be fished quite deep using the bell sinker and three-way swivel set-up. In fact, the lure can be successfully used down to 30 feet or more. The large No. 18 Rapala—original floating model—is best here. A heavy bell sinker of over an ounce may be necessary to ensure contact with the bottom. To find the walleyes a systematic method of slow trolling should be employed. The fish most likely will be schooled along the deeper structure near breaks or slight changes in the regular drop-off.

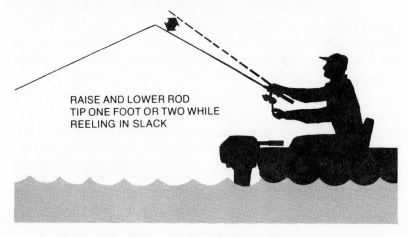

RAISE AND LOWER ROD
TIP ONE FOOT OR TWO WHILE
REELING IN SLACK

Once a school is found, casting shallow and working the Rapala slowly down the break is a good way to work the school of fish thoroughly.

Pumping the lure periodically is often quite effective.The rod tip should be raised a foot or two and as you lower it back reel in the slack before another lift is made. It is most important to keep a taut line while pumping. Otherwise, you may miss many fish. This pumping technique also can be used while trolling.

The heavy weight makes the Rapala plummet toward the bottom on the drop and this is when the walleyes will usually strike the lure. When trolling with this pumping method, try to keep the lure as close to the boat as possible. It is much easier to control in deep water and let's you know where your lure is in relation to the boat.

In the fall, walleye movements are very inconsistent, especially after the fall turnover. On some lakes, they can be located in depths anywhere from two to 70 feet! But there is a certain time when they can be easily found. When frogs migrate back into the lakes to hibernate, walleyes will move into the shallows. This is a brief period but there are major fall walleye runs on lakes that contain tullibees or other members of the whitefish family. In fall, tullibees spawn. This usually starts around late October when the water temperature gets below 40 degrees F.

Tullibees spawn at night over gravel and rubble bottom in about four to six feet of water. If you can locate these spawning areas, you should be in for some fantastic fishing. A good way to find these areas is to run quickly through the shallow, gravel areas shining a powerful flashlight into the water. When you see the silver eyes and gleaming bodies of these small fish, you've found the right areas.

Trolling runs can then be made through the spawning site, but very slowly with large Rapalas with some weight attached. Rapalas are very similar in appearance to the tullibees and for that reason are much more effective than other lures at this time of year. Many big walleyes are taken in this way during the cold water period at night.

Another very effective method is to wade into the water and cast out toward deep water along these spawning grounds.

Retrieve the lure toward shore. This method will not spook the walleyes as much as boat trolling. It also is a very interesting way to fish at night and allows you to cover the spawning site thoroughly. Of course, this should only be attempted in areas where you know the bottom conditions.

During the day, the walleyes will tend to be much deeper but still near the hard-bottom spawning areas. Trolling runs should be made at various depths until a productive pattern is found. It is important to remember that walleyes can scatter at different depths. If, at this time, you only take one or two fish at a certain depth, do not let it mislead you. Keep on experimenting until a more productive pattern is uncovered. Walleyes can be taken in this manner all the way up to the lake's freeze.

Rapalas also are deadly in rivers, especially during the spring and fall. In the early season, when walleyes are in the spawn or post-spawn periods, some very nice catches can be made on Rapalas.

Walleyes can be found along rip-rap banks and flooded shorelines that are near the main river channel. Also, manmade wing-dams and natural points or projections provide excellent walleye structure on rivers as long as they are not too far from the main river channel.

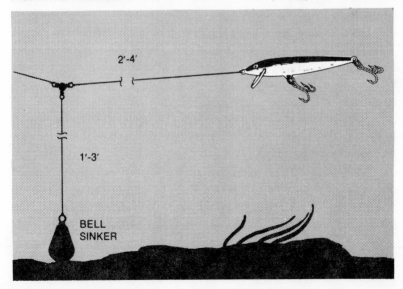

2'-4'

1'-3'

BELL
SINKER

The fish generally will be anywhere from four to 15 feet at this time of year with most of the fish between eight and 12 feet. Look for the washout areas behind these projections. These will usually contain schools, while scattered fish will spread across the shallower areas. I prefer the three-way swivel rig and Rapala at this time of year because the current is usually strong. Trolling runs should be made into the current for proper boat and lure control. Various depths should be run until a successful presentation is established.

When the fish are pinpointed in a small site such as a washout or the tip of a wing-dam, an anchoring and casting approach will work best. You should, however, anchor above the site so that you will be retrieving into the current. A small area can then be thoroughly covered by fan-casting. The retrieve should be as slow as possible, because the walleyes will be quite inactive and unwilling to chase after a lure under these cold water conditions.

When the river water warms and the current subsides, walleyes go into their summer pattern. Generally, they will move out and school in the deep areas of the main river channel. The fish will work the pieces of structure that extend into the channel. Sometimes, they may be suspended in the middle of the channel itself. The method of taking suspended fish discussed earlier can be used here as well.

Deep trolling with large Rapalas is best when they are rigged with the three-way swivel and weight. Check out deep areas and the washouts directly below the dam. This is usually the deepest site in the river and walleyes will gather there during the hot summer months.

In fall, walleyes will generally move shallow again for a time and can be taken with the methods previously discussed for springtime river fishing.

The Rapala is an excellent choice for northern pike too. Its shape and enticing action makes it a natural. In the early part of the year look for northerns along bars that have newly emerging weed growths. When the young "cabbage" weeds are coming up, pike can be taken by trolling over the tops of the weeds with large Rapalas with some weight attached. Random trolling over the very tops of weedy points and sunken islands is very effective.

About 50 feet of line should be let out and your trolling speed should be varied until the proper speed is found for the conditions present.

As the season progresses and the water warms, the northern pike will move out to the deep edges of the weed breaks. The thickest patches of cabbage weeds usually will be the best sites, provided they are on good structure with a fairly quick drop-off. The Deep-Diver Rapalas are a good choice in this case. A method called speed-trolling will trigger the northerns into striking, even when they are not actively feeding.

The trick, however, is to locate the edge of the weeds along a point, sunken island or other good structure. A fairly stiff rod should be used with tough, non-stretch line. Let out from 75 to 100 feet of line and troll very quickly (about 5 mph) along the edge of the weeds, following the contour closely with your fish locator.

Strikes will most often take place when you round a corner, or when the lure reaches a niche in the weedline. Successive trolling runs along a productive weedline will result in bonus large-mouth bass along with the northerns. If there are small, irregular cuts in the weedline that make accurate trolling difficult, casting will work better since you can cast into the weeds and work out, covering the weed edge and the drop-off after it thoroughly. Muskies also can be taken using these same methods.

Early in fall, when the weeds begin turning brown, northern pike will move up into the weedbeds for a feeding binge. Look for the large, flat weed bars with extensive cabbage weedbeds that are still green. Big pike will move up into them in loose groups. Here, a large, floating No. 18 Rapala should be used with very little weight if any. Let out between 25 and 30 feet of line and troll the lure quickly over the weed tops. It should run at a depth of only two or three feet. Jerk the lure hard whenever a weed is felt to rip through it.

Trolling runs also can be made along the sides. Certain weed patches will be more productive than others and your trolling speed should vary until a successful one is found.

Later in fall, in the latter part of October, the pike will again move up, this time to feed on the spawning tullibees if they exist in the lake you are fishing. Seek out those spawning areas described earlier. The same methods of trolling and casting also will work for northerns in this situation. The fish, however, will be found in the deeper water near the spawning site. Again, the large Rapalas will work best since they simulate the spawning forage fish.

The Rapala is an extremely versatile lure that can be used in many other ways to take northern pike. Experiment to find new ways of rigging and working with them.

In smaller sizes, Rapalas are an excellent choice for both large-mouth and smallmouth bass. They can be trolled or cast along weedbeds for largemouth and pitched onto rocky shelves for smallmouth.

Most species of fish are vulnerable to this fine bait fish imitation and the lure's uses are limited only by an angler's imagination.

Editors' Note: Al Lindner has prepared a FREE full color pamphlet for you that is "chock full" of maps, charts, photos and drawings . . This pamphlet tells you about one of the most exciting angling experiments ever attempted or accomplished. The fishing breakthroughs made by Al and his IN'FISHERMAN Staff are making fishing history. To receive this pamphlet and its absolutely free, simply send a 13c stamped self addressed envelope to the IN'FISHERMAN
    Box 999 RW
    Brainerd, MN 56401

RAY OSTROM

*Ray Ostrom began fishing muskies almost 35 years ago, traveling
the 175 miles from his native Minneapolis to Hayward, Wisconsin,
any way that he could, to fish the legendary (and then much more
virginal) Chippewa Flowage. To defray expenses, he would camp
out on an island. That tells us volumes about Ray's dedication. In
the interim, he has become a top officer in the firm that distributes
Rapalas. As a consequence, he has had the opportunity to angle
for most species of gamefish in many parts of the world. But
somehow, he keeps coming back to muskies.*

*Although Ray is modest on the subject, friends reckon that he
has caught and returned more than 100 muskies weighing over
20 pounds. He does have a few on the wall, including the 33-
pounder that captured one of the two international invitational
muskie tournaments Ray has won. There were three such derbies
in all.*

*Ray Ostrom is also a pioneering innovator in fishing education.
He introduced his old friend, Buck Perry to the Upper Midwest
more than 15 years ago. They have remained fast fishing friends.
Ray, like Buck, is always glad to share his encyclopedic know-how;
this time about muskies.*

PERFORMING MUSKIE MAGIC

The word "muskie" is magic to tens of thousands of fishermen, although this species is only found in certain areas of North America. The name sends shivers and creates goose pimples on those of us who seek it, like some kind of magic. Muskie fishing can be compared to tracking a deer all day and seeing only some tracks. A muskie can be a gray ghost appearing as a shadow behind your lure only to fade and disappear, making you talk to yourself and wonder if you really saw something after all. His unpredictability, scarcity and the frustrations he causes bring me and my fellow muskie fishermen back, again and again, to match wits with this trophy fish.

Regardless of size, he *is* a trophy. Hopefully, in a few paragraphs, I can help you catch one of these trophy fish by my hard-won experience. I have been hunting these ghosts for over thirty years and in no way could I count the thousands of hours of determined angling I've spent in seeking this trophy fish. I have had another distinct advantage during my long muskie-hunting career. That was the opportunity of fishing or spending time with the greatest authorities on this species: Cal Johnson, Art Lawton, Louis Spray, all world record holders; Phil Johnson, Bobbie Valdervelden, Tony Burmek, Dan McGuire, Ron Weber, Mike Baranowski, Lou Hanna, Clayt Becker, all tops in the field of catching muskies; and Buck Perry who taught my fishing associates and me the importance of structure fishing.

The true (non-hybrid) muskellunge consists of three recognized sub-species with overlapping ranges and descriptions. Thus, the *tiger*, or *northern*, muskie of Minnesota, Wisconsin, Michigan and western Ontario might possess an almost infinite variety of colorations and markings, ranging from dark-on-light stripes to a dull, solid silver. Similar variations occur among the other two sub-species, the *Great Lakes* muskellunge, and his southern cousin, the *Chautauqua* or *Ohio* muskie. But for the true muskie addict, those differences are only skin deep and do not alter the common viciousness of these killin' cousins.

(Editors' Note: Recently, some experts have begun to question whether there are, indeed, true sub-species of the muskellunge, or whether the variations noted above are only surface differences arising from the coloration of local waters, distinctive regional habitats, etc. Research on the question is now under way. Some new answers might be forthcoming soon.)

I am a firm believer that monster muskies come from large waters. Smaller muskie lakes will produce many fish, but not the huge wallhangers. By wallhangers and monsters, I mean fish in the 30-pound-and-over bracket. This is the fish that I will be relating to in the following paragraphs. Lakes with large numbers of smaller muskies are not a sincere challenge. In no way am I trying to put down the smaller muskie. As I mentioned above, any muskie, regardless of size, is a trophy. However, the large bodies of water, whether a large river or lake, is where the supreme test occurs.

The lures used are of number one importance. Of all of them on the market designed for this species of fish, if I had to choose one, it would be the Rapala, without exception. Keep in mind that a muskie of the size I am talking about is more than likely 12 years of age or over and is more than careful about what he selects for lunch. This does not mean that I don't use something else under certain conditions. For example, if I had a situation of shallow water over logs or a weedbed, I would use either a noisy top-water bait walking on the surface or a bucktail worked with a high rod tip and sputtering on the surface. However, when I do encounter this type of situation and before I would consider going top-water, I would carefully look it over. If there was an open area between the weeds or logs where I could make a cast with a Rapala, I would explore this before I went top-water. In any reef fishing, whether it be rock, weed or stumps, I would use the #18 regular floating Rapala. This 7-inch lure can be fished from depths of one to four feet very easily by varying the speed of retrieve. I have been convinced hundreds of times by the ferociousness of the strike that the muskie was completely fooled by the lifelike action of the Rapala.

The next time you attach a Rapala to your line, watch its action in the water. It not only swims, but it rolls from side to side as it swims. This is true lifelike action. (How many times have you seen a school of minnows swimming and, if you watch carefully, you will notice a few of them flashing because they are rolling slightly side to side. If you are ever fortunate enough to watch a predator fish stalk a school of forage fish, he gets all turned on when one starts to roll slightly and will pass up others to get this particular one. This slight roll is built into a Rapala by design and is not accidental.)

The #18 Rapala floater is my number one choice. It is ideal for the waters I spend most of my time on. It can be worked at extreme slow speeds because of its light balsa construction for top water and is perfectly balanced so it can be speed trolled or retrieved. The #13 and #18 Countdown Magnum models work perfectly for casting or trolling the deep sides of the bars or reefs. I use the Rapala Deep-Diver series for walking the sides of the bars or when speed-trolling structure and tips of bars in 12 to 15 feet of water.

I will describe the perfect northern area waters muskies prefer and how I would fish it. First, I would look for a rock reef within a few hundred yards of a shallow bay. This reef should be close to deep water to allow an escape route for the muskie, some underwater weeds for cover, and a stand of cane weeds to indicate some hard sand bottom. To make this a 100 per cent ideal area, I would like a beaver house close to the shallow bay area. The beaver, in making his house, has dragged a lot of brush and logs to the vicinity, making this a natural place for bait fish to hide. I would approach this area very quietly by shutting off my motor a hundred yards or more away from the reef and use the wind to drift the boat into a casting position. Running your motor up to

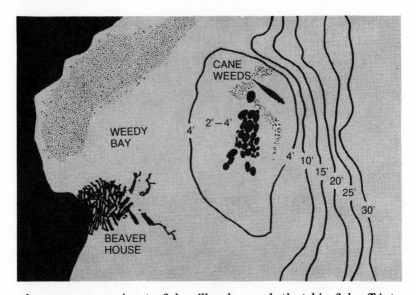

where you are going to fish will only spook that big fish off into deep water. As the boat approaches within casting distance, I would use the #18 regular floating model Rapala and watch carefully for the formation of underwater weeds to place the cast without getting hung up. As I described, the cane weeds, indicating sand and gravel below, should be worked with accurate, systematic casting. It may only be a small section of the reef, but this is a consistently productive spot for large fish. Work slowly and meticulously by paddling quietly around the reef, keeping the distance of a cast away. Periodically turn your back on the reef and cast toward the open water. There is a chance that a good fish may have spooked from the reef or weed bed and has moved out in the deeper water. You should then work the beaver house, fishing your way over to it. After working over the beaver house, you should then fish the rest of the bay. Although the reef is the muskie's home, he may be out roaming the bay in what we call "shopping." After you are convinced that nobody's home, go back and troll the deep water side of the reef with the #18 Countdown Rapala.

Other areas that should be worked—and basically in the same manner — are the points of shorelines and islands. Remember, however, that the value of the area is measured by the under-

water weed bed, cane weeds, brush and rocks. Keep in mind, especially, underwater rock structure in relation to the weeds. Shallow-water weedy bays without a reef may produce a few fish in the spring of the year; but for warm weather, middle and late summer fishing, your success will be greatly increased under the conditions described above.

The mouths of rivers and streams are of significant import-ance to a muskie. This is an area that seems to be extremely attractive to him. It is more than likely he frequents this area because it attracts many small fish, making it easy to get a meal. Here, again, the #18 regular floating Rapala can't be beat. It is a natural. Another good thing about this type of area is that it is not particularly affected by weather conditions or time of day as much as other areas of the lake.

Weather conditions and the time of day do mean 90 per cent of fishing success for muskies. The ideal conditions would be the advent of a low pressure area with heavy overcast and warm temperature. Add just a little mist or slight amount of warm rain off and on during the day, plus just enough wind to drift the boat slowly, and you'll have just the kind of day on which to see that huge gray ghost following your lure on any cast.

The worst conditions are under a bright, hot sun during the middle of summer with no wind. Under these conditions, you should start your fishing before daylight and fish until about 9 a.m., relax, entertain your family or play gin; and start fishing again about 7 p.m. and work the known hot spots until after dark, or when the bugs drive you off the lake. Yes, muskies will hit after dark and I'm convinced this is an ideal time. There are no sun rays, motor noises or other disturbances to chase them out of the shallows. When it gets late in the evening and the water quiets down, a slowly worked #18 floating Rapala with just the tail section breaking the surface, or a top-water lure could produce the trophy fish you are looking for.

The best time of the year to consistently catch large muskies has, for me, been early fall when the leaves are turning and the weeds in the lake are dying and the surface temperatures are cooling. The fish still frequent the same areas, but stay shallower for longer periods of time. They are more eager to follow and take a lure even at the rod tip on a figure 8. "Figure 8'ing" is a very

important part of muskie fishing and should be practiced so it can be done in perfect rhythm. On every cast, your eye should constantly track the lure to watch for *any* indication of a follow. If you see, or even *think* you see, something, *do not stop your lure.* Speed it up gradually to a high speed and, as it approaches the boat, put your rod down into the water to a depth of about two feet. Keep reeling the lure to the very tip. Now keep the lure in motion by moving the rod in the form of a figure 8 so that it *does not stop or even hesitate.* If the muskie's interest has really been aroused, he will stay after the lure. After you make a large figure 8, switch to a circle, then go back to a figure 8, putting your rod deeper into the water. Don't stop just because he disappears! More than likely, when he "disappeared," he was hiding in the shadow of your boat. There have been many trophy muskies taken on a figure 8 and when it happens to you, it will remind you of a large dog grabbing a stick our of your hand. Keep your rod deep in the water until he strips off some line and don't be surprised if he completely clears the water in his first leap only a few feet from your boat.

After you have thoroughly worked a sighted fish and have not been able to make a hook-up, let him rest. Leave for about half-an-hour and then come back. Try again. If you fail to raise him on the second try, leave him alone. But, whenever you go by this particular spot, fish it. A sighted fish means the conditions of the area are right and could always be a potential fish producer.

I disagree with the belief that muskies are loners. On one small reef one evening, my fishing partners and I raised five huge fish from 25 to 40 pounds. We had three of them following and chasing our figure 8'd Rapalas at one time! After three return trips to the same spot that evening, we boated and released two in the 35-pound class. We have since named this spot "Grandma's Bar," appropriately, because of the residents living there.

Another instance of schooled muskies happened two years ago when we hooked, boated and released three in thirty minutes in less than a 100-square-foot area.

I mention these experiences to tell you that after you have caught a muskie on a spot, it does not mean you should leave. It could produce another, maybe even larger than the one you've just boated.

You should have two rods ready to go at all times. When a fish is spotted, you have to work fast and systematically. For example: When you do have a follow-up to your boat and are unseccessful in making him strike on the figure 8, you should cast back to the area where you originally raised him. After 4 or 5 casts in that general area without a sighting, switch to the other rod with a

RAY OSTROM

different color Rapala. This quick change is necessary to keep the muskie's interest. Chances are that he will be turned on only for a few seconds and a complete plan of systematic action is necessary to convert that follow into a strike.

I also strongly suggest that *several times a day* you cut off the last two or three feet of your line, discard in the litter bag, and retie the knot. Most line abrasion occurs at the tip guide although new ceramic technologies have greatly reduced the wear, tear and scoring caused by even the hardest metallic guides. And it's never a bad idea to periodically scrutinize *all* of your guides for minute cracks, nicks and imperfections.

For equipment in fishing large muskies, I prefer using a casting reel with an anti-reverse and star drag. Spinning reels can be used, but I feel the advantage of the shorter, stiffer rod is a "must" to figure 8 properly, when it is important to control the speed of the lure. Also, for setting the hook and holding a large fish, I much prefer a rod of about 5½ feet (certainly not over 6 feet) in a medium to medium-heavy action.

Since monofilament has been refined, I use it exclusively and in nothing heavier than 17-pound test. I tie directly to a fairly heavy lock snap—no leader. The Rapala is a truly balanced lure, being individually hand-tested and balanced at the factory for perfect swimming action. Any hardware-like leaders, ball-bearing swivels or *any* swivel, for that matter, placed in front of the Rapala will take away from its lifelike action. It is necessary, however, when not using a leader to make every effort to hold a hooked muskie's head high, to keep the line away from his mouth full of razor blades.

When using the floating model Rapalas for casting, alter the speed of the retrieves, making some slow, others fast. About half way through the retrieve, increase the speed as you would when you had a follow. Every once in a while, make a figure 8, even if you don't see a follow. It's good practice and you may have had a fish move to the shadow of the boat, out of your vision.

My associates and I prefer to cast for our muskies. The waters we are fishing can be worked more thoroughly by casting and we enjoy it more than trolling. Trolling, however, is very seccessful in some areas and is almost a must under some conditions. Large rivers such as the St. Lawrence, for example, would be difficult to work the same way as we fish our waters. Here, again, structure is important and knowing your waters is of extreme importance to success. Rivers or lakes; the challenge is there and the muskie is king!

In darker muskie waters, I prefer the gold Rapala; choosing silver or blue in clear waters. In late spring, just after muskies are through spawning, the gold/fluorescent red is excellent.

Muskie addicts are trophy fishermen and, in the eyes of some, they are "a couple bricks short of a full load." They will fish for days and go home happy to talk about a splash or a shadow or two they might have seen behind their lure. Most significant about the true muskie fisherman is his admiration for this fish. After he has spent days to catch one, he will admire it and then release it.

The true muskie fisherman must be compared to the sail and marlin fishermen when it comes to releasing. No muskie fisherman would deny his partner or himself a trophy for the wall; but, if the fish is not going on the wall, he would rather see it released than killed. The muskie is truly a prized fish and is anything but plentiful. Hopefully, every new muskie fisherman will take this same attitude to assure posterity that these giants of the freshwater will always be here.

Today, the knowledge of fish habits and movement has been proved and documented by many professionals through the use of science and modern technology. Despite all of this information, there are still large gray areas in which there are no answers in regard to catching the muskie. We know some of his habits and some of his movements, but they are a minor part of his life. Maybe we would rather not know. The challenge in trying to figure out this fish is reward enough.

For old and new muskie fishermen alike, there are now numerous clubs in which muskie enthusiasts can get together and swap tales and help the species.

Following is a list of muskie clubs. One may be in your area:

Muskies, Inc.
(Gil Hamm, founder)
1708 University Avenue
St. Paul, Minnesota 55104
(612) 644-8684

(Editors' Note: This is the seminal organization which now boasts over 2,500 members in 27 states and Canada. They have planted 27,700 yearling 12-inch muskies in 40 lakes since the club's founding in 1966. MI owns and operates an $80,000 muskie hatchery and rearing complex at Battle Lake, Minnesota.)

Fargo-Moorhead Chapter of MI
(Bob Schmidt, regional vice president)
94 Woodcrest Drive, South
Fargo, North Dakota 58102
(701) 237-0940

Muskie Hunters, Illinois, Chapter of MI
(Larry Ramsell, regional vice president)
446 North Cedar
Galesburg, Illinois 61401
(309) 343-0482

Pomme de Terre, Missouri, Chapter of MI
(John Stueber, Sr., regional vice president)
Pittsburg, Missouri 65724
(417) 852-4595

First, Wisconsin, Chapter of MI
(Elmo Korn, regional vice president)
525 Woodward Avenue
Chippewa Falls, Wisconsin 54729
(715) 723-9548

Bill's Muskie Club
C/O Bill Hoeft
932 South Third Avenue
Wausau, Wisconsin 54401

Blackhawk Muskie Association
PO Box 664
Janesville, Wisconsin 53545

Iowa Great Lakes Muskie Club
PO Box 148
Royal, Iowa 51357

Husky Musky Club of West Virginia
3511 Randolph Drive
Parkersburg, West Virgina 26101

Kentucky Silver Muskie Club
6804 Mariposa Drive
Louisville, Kentucky 40214

Michigan-Ontario Muskie Association
C/O Homer LeBlanc
23323 Liberty
St. Clair Shores, Michigan 48080

Muskellunge Club of Wisconsin
3451 North 95th Street
Milwaukee, Wisconsin 53222

Wisconsin Muskies, Ltd.
PO Box 502
Waukesha, Wisconsin 53186

Pennsylvania Muskie Society
701 Yardley Commons
Yardley, Pennsylvania 19067

Project Illini
5612 West 127th Street
Palos Heights, Illinois 60463

(Editors' note: Our apologies if we have inadvertently missed your muskie club. Please advise us at Normark Corporation and we will see that you are included in the next edition of this book!)

RAY JOHNSON

*Like an 8.0 quake on the Richter Scale, Ray Johnson rocked the
national fishing establishment to its very foundations early
in 1976 with the publication, in the February edition of SPORTS
AFIELD magazine, of the story, "How to Catch Super Trout."
The message was: troll the #11 Countdown Rapala very slowly at
night in shallow water close to shore of lakes or impoundments
holding large German brown trout.*

*No sooner had the story been published than Ray immediately
increased the tremors by going out and establishing a new
world's record, catching a 26 lb., 4 oz., brown in Utah's suddenly
famous (thanks mainly to Johnson himself) Flaming Gorge
Reservoir on six-pound-test line. And that's not the end of it:
since publication of the first story on Rapalas and the big cannibals of Flaming Gorge, Ray has caught a half-dozen more there in
the 20-lb. class, and a 15 lb., 7 oz., brown on two-pound-test line,
breaking the old world's record for the same class line by almost
seven pounds. Sadly, Ray tells of losing at the boat a brown that
certainly would have exceeded 35 lbs., proving that he's human,
after all! In this story, Ray gives us a definitive account of his
revolutionary way of catching trophy trout with the Rapala.*

CATCHING LARGE TROPHY TROUT

Extensive field testing over many years has proven conclusively that by far more large trout (and many other species) will bite on Rapala lures, consistently, than on any other lure ever devised and available. I have exhaustively used all of the following in direct comparison, side by side, for literally thousands of hours: spinners, spoons, "banana"-type plugs, clothespin lures, wobblers in addition to the many *imitation* Rapalas, even jigs (some effective lures for trout . .) and proven over and over again to myself and others that far more large trout will readily take Rapalas than all of these other lures combined.

That is quite a statement. What verification? In easily accessible U.S. public trout waters where virtually tens of thousands of fishermen use every type of lure and bait and fly available year-round, the Rapala has built a living legend of catching 8 and 9 and 10 yr. old trout *almost every day* (most over 10 lbs.- many near and over 20 lbs., to 32 lbs.) . . . while none or very few such trout are caught on all other lures and baits combined, *during each whole year!*

I, personally, have caught and helped others fishing with me catch thousands of trout over 5 lbs. and hundreds of trout over 8 lbs. (more than a hundred over 10 lbs. to 30 lbs.). The Rapala has fooled so many of these large trophy trout that credit has been given to it for having helped me catch far more large trout from public waters than have ever been caught before *on anything* by anyone.

I have caught over 40 trout from public waters which each weighed more than 10 lbs. *within just a two month period* . . . on Rapalas. I have caught six different trout over 10 lbs. *in one day*, and five other trout over 10 lbs. each *in one day* . . . on Rapalas.

I have caught trout of all four species present, each over 10 lbs., *in one day*, twice (browns, cut throats, rainbows and lake trout)... on Rapalas. But, through all the years I've tried, I've never succeeded in doing any of these things on *any other lure or bait* (including real minnows). And, again, I've tried everything else very extensively.

With many fishing partners, trading off and utilizing every technique of retrieve, I have seen virtually every large trout take the Rapala rather than anything else we've been simultaneously using, many dozens of times over many years. I can and do catch unusually large trophy-sized trout consistently, year after year, on most days I fish with Rapalas. I seldom catch any large trout of any real size on any day when I'm using anything else. I can catch lots of trout of truly large size on Rapalas—I do! I catch hardly any truly large-sized trout on any of the many other things I've exhaustively used. I try, but I don't.

Why? Is the Rapala really more attractive, appealing or provocative to large trout than any other lure or bait? Yes! The answer is definitely "yes". Most exaggerated answers to the endless fisherman's dream of how to catch more and larger fish are simply untrue sales gimmicks and will *not* in actual usuage catch many more or much larger fish than anything else you've already tried. Most miracle lures prove in real life fishing to actually catch *fewer* and *smaller* fish than the old stand-bys you already use.

The preceeding list of good trout lures, and some others, will sometimes catch a large trout and will often catch lots of smaller fish. But, despite their effectiveness and appearances in record books and fishing contests, the Rapala will consistently catch far more large trout than any of the others. I have proven it in my own fishing, by racking up the most impressive and successful trophy-trout catching record in history. You can prove it to yourself, also, by learning to use Rapalas correctly and then using them consistently (with many other species of fish, also, in addition to trout).

Here's how. Have patience. Persevere—continue using the Rapalas constantly, despite any apparent lack of results. Fish for larger fish than are normally caught where you're fishing. Realize that there often aren't as many large fish present in a given body of water as there are small ones. So you may not catch very many fish very fast. *Don't* fall into the trap of giving up on the large fish if you don't catch anything. Don't quit using the Rapalas and start using something else. You won't prove a thing (or likely catch many large fish) if you don't keep the Rapalas on and in intensive use. Don't be tempted to fish for small fish with bait or little lures. Large trout in most waters *will all* try to eat Rapala lures when they are hungry if the Rapala is near them and appears natural. All it means when you fail to get any strikes on Rapalas is either that hungry fish are not seeing the Rapala or you aren't fishing it correctly. Large trout will strike the Rapala as if to eat it when hungry. All you have to do is to "feed" it to the trout, when and where and how they want to eat it.

Some fishermen believe in moving lures and baits fast— others slowly. Many want to believe that they can make a fish bite or strike when it isn't hungry or feeding. Overcoming the many frequent periods of time when most fish simply are not hungry and pay no attention to any and all food around them. Limited success with some species is achieved by moving a lure, bait or fly quickly at a fast pace—apparently arousing some instinct within the fish to strike out suddenly, involuntarily without planning to. This seldom attracts strikes from brown, cut-throat, rainbow, brook or lake trout of very large size, however. It usually only works with small trout.

Also, countless anglers love to jerk and wiggle a bait or lure, exaggerating its own built-in movement, thinking that it helps make their hook look like an injured minnow, etc., and believing that a fish will more readily eat an injured-appearing minnow than a healthy looking one. Sometimes, with fish such as northern pike, this may seem to work. But, seldom does it seem to attract any more strikes from large trout on Rapalas (or most other lures or baits). Fish your Rapalas slowly and steadily. Surprisingly, to me, no one color of Rapalas catches more fish than any other color.

The very reason Rapalas work so much better than any other lure or bait yet devised is because of their unique appearance, shape, movement and vibration. To a fish, especially a large trout, the Rapala is the most realistic appearing lure yet devised. Its shape and subtle movements look more like a real live small fish to a large trout than any bait, fly, lure or dead minnow. It's as simple as that .... and true.

And don't believe that large trout prefer insects, crawfish, cheese, worms or shrimp to eat. In most waters, this simply isn't true. Nearly all trout over 5 lbs., and most over 3 lbs., eat mostly smaller fish and minnows, if available, in the waters where they live—both streams and lakes. Occasionally, large trout can be caught on things other than minnow-imitations and real small fish. I've caught many trout over 10 lbs., from public waters on flies (some small flies). And it is fun. Also, glutton rainbows will sometimes still eat cheese, even after they grow quite large. But these are all the occasional exceptions, not the rule. Nearly all large trout everywhere eat mostly only smaller fish. And few waters that harbor many trout of any size lack an adequate population of smaller fish for the trout to feed and grow on.

The Rapala most closely resembles, of all lures and baits, the daily food of most large trout. They will, and do, therefore, try to eat it more often than any other object in their environment.

Much of the Rapala's effectiveness is due to its lack of exaggerated movement (subtle shimmying rather than lots of darting and wild wiggling). Watch a small fish swim. Its body moves gently. Most lures wiggle, dart or spin much more than a real minnow's body moves. And no other lure, matches the movement and appearance of real fish like Rapalas. Many fish don't care—especially the members of the pike family, bass family and many ocean species. But most large trout *do*. They have been fished for over the years by a vast army of anglers who have used every conceivable kind of bait and lure. But the trout seldom, if ever, tumble for these artificials, which shows us the wariness of these trout.

Large fish of many species, like large trout, are deceived and tempted into trying to eat Rapalas much more easily, consistently and often than into trying to eat anything else we have available to use. These fish grow large only by refusing to eat the many countless offerings presented to them by all the anglers. Rapalas will catch these large, uncaught fish—nearly all of them. No other lure or bait will; short of live minnows (which are illegal in most trout waters and difficult to keep alive and attractive looking, even where allowed).

Another reason large trout and large individuals of many other species are seldom caught by most anglers is because they usually feed at *night*, in the dark—just as most other wildlife

comes out of hiding and resting to feed and move about at night. Most fish are nocturnal—especially large trout such as browns, which live and survive, avoiding getting caught, in heavily-fished waters. Use Rapalas, which resemble natural prey, at dusk, after dark and at dawn, and you will greatly increase your catch of large trout—because those are the times they are most often active, swimming about looking for something to eat, hungry, and in the mood to pay attention to your hook. Dusk and night fishing is a big key to my success. Most fish can see well enough even on dark nights to feed. They *do* feed at night. They often avoid daytime sunlight and refuse to bite or strike at anything as long as light penetrates the water. Concentrate on nighttime fishing, not daytime fishing.

Depth is another important factor in catching large numbers

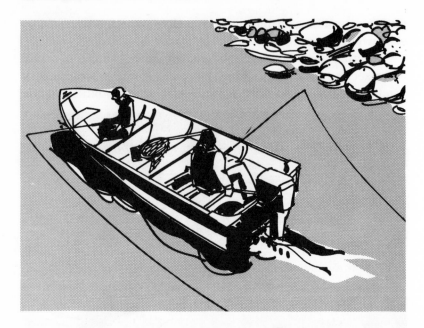

of large trout. Contrary to most opinions, most big trout feed near the surface and near the shoreline in any body of water that is at all deep. Cold and warm water temperatures don't affect this habit of their feeding shallow very much at all, even in the cold of winter and in the hot of summer. They still feed most often near the surface and shoreline in summer—after dark when the sun's rays are gone. In winter, they like, not dislike, the surface layers of water. Those who fish with me catch more large trout within a few feet of the shoreline, in just a few feet of water, than all of the other fishermen combined catch from all the rest of the waters we fish (summer and winter). Lake trout are not really trout, and are one exception, in that they often *do* feed quite deep and live quite deep much of the year in many waters.

Most large trout slowly sneak up from beneath on an unsuspecting small fish swimming *above* their head. They gently grab it sideways in their mouth to kill it—then turn it and swallow it head first. Several things can be learned by the observant fisherman from this feeding trait. Large trout look for an easy-to-catch meal when hungry—not a fast moving hard-to-catch meal. They do not often chase your Rapala down, but rather sneak up on it from below. The way they take it produces only a light bite or strike—not a hard one. And they quickly spit it out once they determine that it is not the "real thing". *When using Rapalas, jerk on strike quickly at any and all "touches", however soft. Large trout seldom hook themselves.*It is wise to carefully pay attention to your line at all times, and react instantly. Otherwise, many, if not most, large trout which do bite will not get hooked or caught, even when they do bite. Rapala trebles effectively hook and hold even the largest trout very well, as long as you do your part and react quickly and then play the fish correctly (keeping enough tension to prevent hooks from loosening, but not so tight as to risk line breakage). When using Rapalas, many of those "soft" bites you get are actually the largest trout striking. The "hard" bites are generally only small trout.

Small diameter lines, premium monofilaments, greatly help to fool and catch large trout. The lighter test, the smaller diameter are less noticeable to these large trout which have not ever fallen to any other fishermen's lures. I personally use 6 lb. test most often, catching even my 20 lb. to 30 lb. trout on it. Light lines also enable the lure to move most easily and naturally. They will produce far more strikes from large trout than will heavier lines.

A small snap or ring attached to the eye of the Rapala allows free movement of the lure. However, I usually tie the Rapala directly to my line—feeling that some large trout might shy away from any unnatural hardware—even a small snap or ring. A strong knot which does not weaken the line is mandatory when catching large fish on light test lines.

The fun and unparalleled success of using light test monofilament lines to catch fish, whether large or small, should be taught to children as well as to all adults. Using heavy gear, tackle, popgear, etc., is not only unnecessary but also detrimental to both results and enjoyment. If more people would use light tackle and lines, more fish would actually be caught—and far more large trout. The Rapala is the ideal weapon to use on the end of a light line.

Trout will eat every size of Rapala, from the smallest to the largest they can get in their mouth. However, smaller Rapalas generally bring more strikes from small to medium sized trout than the larger lures. Most minnows and small fish eaten by large trout are the size of shiners, threadfin shad and small rainbows and chubs (3-5 inches). I personally prefer to use Rapalas in those sizes when fishing for large trout. #11 is my favorite size, with #9 my second choice.

Floating models are best for actual surface fishing and extremely shallow areas. They are also best for deep fishing, as they ride up above the bottom behind heavy gear. The Countdown sinking models are my most frequent choice, since they ride a few feet under the surface when trolled, and will sink for controlled depth fishing. Large trout often wait 10-15 feet under the surface along the shoreline for small fish to swim over them when feeding. The sinking models ride just over their heads within easy reach.

As you might expect, I troll for these large trout. Trolling, as done at Flaming Gorge, is a difficult and demanding art, vastly different from the way most people conceive of it. I guide the boat very slowly along the shores and banks, practically on the banks, following the contours of the shoreline, keeping my Rapala working ten to 12 feet under the surface, just over the rocks and bushes and logs right next to shore.

The ideal habitat for large trout on Flaming Gorge, and very probably on your big trout lake, seems to include several elements. I feel that certain combinations of rocks, boulders, gravel, cliffs and/or bushes (with moss, snails, shrimp and bug hatches) extending along the shore from the waterline down the sloping sides under the water to 30 or 40 feet are these absolutely necessary elements.

Because Flaming Gorge has very steep banks, most of the time I can literally touch the banks with my rod tip as I troll. This requires constant attention and skillful boat handling. Keeping the lure working that close to both the shore and the bottom without constantly hanging up is difficult and demanding. Yet, if I move even a few feet farther from shore, I catch much, much less.

All I feel when these huge trout hit is either a gentle bump, a pull or slack line, and then only for an instant. If I feel anything, I immediately jerk back hard. Even so, most of the largest and wariest trout have already detected the sharp hooks and the artificial lure and have opened their mouths to expel the Rapala. Most large trout I catch are hooked by the lip!

In addition to using a sufficiently light line and fishing at the proper depth, speed and distance from the shoreline, it is *imperative that when angling this way, you constantly hold your rod ready to strike every instant the Rapala is in the water.* My arm is coiled like a rattlesnake ready to strike, every second. It's the only way to hook and catch very many of these large trout. A fishing rod leaning against the gunwhale or held by a rod-holder just won't do the job. You, the alert and dedicated angler, *have* to set the hook.

When setting the hook, I jerk fast and hard and start reeling fast and furiously, and run toward the front of the boat—to set the hook, take up the slack and stretch the line. In addition to being hard for the fish to detect, monofilament line prevents most break-offs at this juncture because of its stretch. So if you're properly rigged, don't hesitate to set the hook just as I've described. The mark of a good trout fisherman, after all, is his ability to set the hook consistently in the soft takers, because they are usually the largest trout.

Any mistake in playing these big fish will lose them rather quickly. Many are lost at boatside during the netting attempt. I never put the net into the water, or even over the side of the boat, until the last second before netting the fish. I make one deep jab with the net under the fish in front of its snout, so that it swims right into the net.

I literally catch so many trout of such large size on Rapalas, that I'm known for having had more trout mounted for display than anyone else. Plus, when fishing, I often catch far too many large fish to keep—because of limits and practicality. Since I enjoy catching these beautiful trophy fish so thoroughly, I like to preserve those which I keep for others to see and enjoy. I release unharmed all of those which I don't care to have mounted for display. I seldom keep any trout under 14 lbs. anymore. I actually catch so many trout larger than that, that I enjoy letting even 12 lbers. go to grow larger and be caught again. Releasing fish we catch, is the easiest, cheapest way to assure ourselves and others of good fishing when we return again to fish.

Learn to use Rapalas. Keep using them until you get results. Don't quit when nothing bites. Use light lines; preferably 6 lb. or 8 lb. Work it very slowly, whether casting or trolling. Pull it steadily. There is no need to add action to a Rapala. A steady retrieve usually works best. Be alert. Hold your rod at all times and set the hook immediately when you feel anything. The largest trout usually bite the softest. Fish before the sun comes up and, especially, after it goes down and into the dark. Fish close to banks and shores, close to the surface no deeper than 15 feet (unless in shallow streams). Keep your Rapala's hooks sharp. And replace them whenever bent. Tie Rapalas directly to your monofilament or use a small snap or ring only (no swivel). Fish for large fish, not small, If you do, Rapalas will catch you larger trout than you've ever caught before (and, often, even more small ones).

RON SCHARA

Ron Schara, award-winning outdoor writer for the Minneapolis TRIBUNE, was raised in the limestone bluff-trout stream hill country of northeast Iowa. He was weaned on trout fishing, later to discover the Mississippi River for its walleyes, bass and panfish. In addition to outdoor writing, Ron also received fish and wildlife biology training at Iowa State University.

Now a resident of Minneapolis, Ron has fished the entire length of Minnesota, western Wisconsin and southwestern Ontario, Canada. In addition, he has fished from South America to the Arctic Circle. While he is certainly considered an expert angler, Ron, 33, says he is "still learning and discovering new things about the Great Sport of Angling and picks up something new from every fishing partner."

His hope is that you might pick up a few useful tidbits from his story.

FISHING UP AND DOWN

Many fishermen do it. The ice angler must. But seldom do fishermen really think about vertical fishing. That is—fishing straight up and down.

Angling vertically—to be effective—is a skill of its own when artificial lures are involved. It's one thing to vertically fish with live bait, such as minnows. Not much to it. The minnow provides its own action and a bobber on top usually signals a strike.

But with artificials, such as the specially-designed Rapalas, vertical fishing becomes a new ball game.

A couple of winters ago I took a short fly-in winter fishing trip out of Baudette, Minnesota to the wide frozen flats of Lake of the Woods. The big border lake is noted for its wealth of walleyes and saugers—though not in the trophy category. As often happens in winter, the walleyes were rapping our fathead minnows, running for a few feet, then . . . nothing. The walleyes acted like they were teasing, simply taking the minnow, mouthing it but not feeding. It was frustrating.

But because the walleyes were at least anxious to hit it was time to pull a switch. I tied on the special Solid Lead-bodied Rapala, dropped it to the bottom and jigged the lure. The jigging action, aided by the lure's own design, creates a circular "wounded" minnow act. But at one instant, just as the lure was swinging downward, the tension in my monofilament disappeared. Boom. I snapped back on the line and instantly felt the struggle of a hooked walleye. I managed to take six walleyes within the next 45 minutes—all on the artificial Rapala—whereas earlier we had strikes but no fish.

We'll discuss vertical techniques but first let's go back. When do you fish vertically? In fishing through the ice, you have no

Swimming Action of Balanced Jigging Rapala Covers Large Area

choice, of course. With a 4-inch hole to work in, you must admit it would be a little difficult to cast or troll. Hence you must fish, put action into your lure and land the fish—all up and down.

With those restrictions why would anyone want to fish vertically in open water? Largely for the same reasons as ice fishing: you have no choice. The lake trout fisherman—after the lake surface warms—is faced with reaching his fish at depths which may exceed 100 feet. It's difficult and cumbersome to troll at those depths without dragging a pound of lead or buying down-riggers. Casting is slow and inefficient.

That leaves vertical fishing—where you position your boat over known lake trout hang-outs and fish up and down in the most productive depths.

So—you can see that vertical fishing, though you may not have thought much about it—has a place in the list of multiple skills which an angler should seek to possess. And, as far as deciding when to vertical fish, it is commonsense. Whenever, in any fishing situation, it is impossible to reach your quarry by more conventional methods YOU CAN FISH VERTICALLY AND BE EFFECTIVE. And that goes for nearly every game fish, including some saltwater species that normally hang deep in the ocean depths.

Though bass fishermen seldom think about, the pros will tell you that when the largemouths have moved out of the shallows, vertical fishing with spoons, for example, can be the only technique that'll put fish in the live-well.

Well enough of the sales pitch on vertical angling. Let it be said it's a fish producer if you master a few techniques.

What is a vertical lure? Rapala has two models which represent the two basic vertical techniques. One, the Rapala Balanced jigging lure, is a minnow-looking version, moulded of lead, which

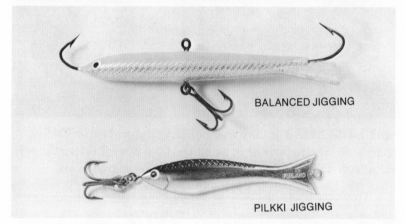

BALANCED JIGGING

PILKKI JIGGING

sets horizontally in the water. Special design makes the Rapala swim in a circular motion when it is jigged upwards and allowed to fall.

The other Rapala is called the "Pilkki" jigging model a spoon-like lure moulded of lead, also specially designed for vertical use. When jigged or vibrated by a thrumming rod, the Pilkki jig quivers much like a dying minnow. It may also be jigged in a sweeping motion and allowed to drop whereby the Pilkki flutters and rocks like injured prey.

Since both lures have built-in actions, the angler need only vary his motion until the action is found that takes fish. It may take experimenting because one particular action pattern will attract strikes one day but not the next.

I remember sitting over a school of crappies on Minnesota's Granite Lake one winter when the Rapala Balanced jigging lure had to be almost still before the slabs would hit. The crappies were suspended under the ice in about 21 feet of water, a fact which

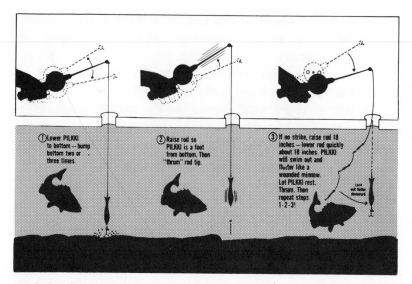

① Lower PILKKI to bottom — bump bottom two or three times

② Raise rod so PILKKI is a foot from bottom. Then "thrum" rod tip.

③ If no strike, raise rod 18 inches — lower rod quickly about 18 inches. PILKKI will swim out and flutter like a wounded minnow. Let PILKKI rest. Thrum. Then repeat steps 1-2-3!

can't be discovered in any manner but trial and error. Or ask. A fisherman who happened to be on the lake when I arrived simply volunteered the key info. If he hadn't I was prepared to ask.

Thinking that the crappies would want something lively and thinking the Rapala would have to be in constant motion, I pumped my ice rod vigorously for several minutes, never letting the lure pause long.

My thinking produced no strikes. So I changed. With the Rapala now relatively still, I tenderly vibrated the line, knowing the lure would go into a light but tantalizing wiggle. Smack the crappie had it. That technique produced a dozen nice-sized slabs that day.

The point here is do not give the vertical working lure an aggressive action, particularly under ice fishing conditions. The water is cold and the cold-blooded crappies, or walleyes or northern pike are equally affected. A fish in an ice-covered lake has a lower metabolism—meaning almost every function is slowed down by the cold water temperatures.

Hence, if you make the lure look to aggressive, to difficult to catch, the fish you are after may look for an easier meal. Another point is that over-aggression by the lure may discourage a strike simply because a crappie or walleye is not about to nab more than it can handle. Its predator instinct says take the path of least resistance, be an opportunist. A lure that acts like it may be tough and hungry may ward off any takers.

Bob Underwood in his book, "Lunker", spent hundreds of hours underwater in scuba gear observing bass. More than once he saw bass pass up a lure because the fisherman had made it appear too strong, too aggressive to attack. Don't make the same mistake in giving action to the jigging Rapala. Make it struggle, squirm, dip and dive but make it look painful or hurt. To do that the lure must pause occasionally as if the bait was weakening and had to rest before struggling to move again.

Most often walleyes, crappies and northern pike (and every other gamefish) will nab a vertically fished lure as the lure is falling. Sometimes the strike will take place as you begin another jigging action but don't count on it. Do be prepared for it, however.

But generally the strike will occur while the Rapala is dropping or just as it reaches the top of its swimming movement.

As a result the greatest challenge in vertical fishing is to consistently detect a strike. The live bait user has no problem because there is more time. Twitch a minnow and the walleye will run away with it and start swallowing. But the artificial Rapala, like any plastic, wood or metal lure, is easily and quickly detected as uneatable. Faster than the eye, a walleye can reject the hooks—unless of course you've already buried the barb. (Without sounding commercial, a fisherman has an added advantage with the Rapala because of the unequalled sharpness of its hooks. As a result, sometimes the hook is buried by the force of the strike alone. But don't let the lure do all the work.)

Because of the nature of the strike—on the fall—the angler is faced with a slack line at the moment the fish inhales the lure. That means the strike is seldom "felt", or detected by any telegraphing through the line.

However—and this is important—most often the strike can be seen. Yes. As a result vertical fishing becomes a line watching affair. And what do you look for? Basically a pause in the line as it descends. If no strike occurs as the Rapala falls the line will smoothly peel off until the lure reaches the end. It's when the line halts abruptly that the strike has occurred. Set the hook immediately. To do so, you may even have to run back from the hole in the ice to take up the slack. Do not expect to feel anything. Chances are you won't.

Vertical Fishing Trophies Caught by Marty Engle, Minneapolis

Fishermen who have sharpened their vertical fishing skills may eventually try jigging a Rapala "with slack but no slack." By that, I mean the lure is raised and lowered as life-like as possible with as little slack in the line as possible. To do it, the angler must concentrate on the length and speed of the jigging action and attempt to adjust the line slack as the lure moves. In this manner, you may achieve a constant "feel" contact with what's happening down below. And more importantly, you'll actually feel the strike as a "tick" on the line. Retaliate immediately.

But don't give up line watching. Certain gamefish, such as the lake trout, will sometimes hit the Rapala from the side while the lure may be swinging. Again you won't feel a thing even with a relatively tight line. You will see the line hesitate, however. Again you must set the hook and be prepared to make the set in a wide arc. If the lake trout nabs the lure from the side and then swims in an upward direction, a short set may never eliminate the slack in the line. Hence, the trout will never feel the hook. By that time the lure probably will be rejected.

Vertical fishing for trout in open water with a long rod partially eliminates the setting problem, of course. The rod should be snapped straight up, not to one side or the other. By raising the rod straight over your head or thereabouts, you have the greatest arc and you've taken up the greatest amount of slack in the line possible. Most often that'll be sufficient to bury the barbs. Be quick about it, though.

The Rapala Pilkki is fished with all of the same principles as the Balanced model. With one exception. The Pilkki may also be dressed up with a touch of live bait whenever necessary. Minnows or ice fishing baits, such as wax worms, often are very effective. In this manner, the Pilkki's tantalizing action acts as an attractor, drawing crappies in, for instance, until a crappie then eyes the minnow. The use of live bait means you can afford to be a little slower on the draw, of course. You'll have more time to set the hook but you'll still have to be a line watcher to readily detect the strike.

You may ask: when using live bait why bother with the Pilkki? Good question. But don't underestimate the Pilkki's contribution as a fish attractor. The lure's metallic finish and unique design gives it the action and looks of a troubled minnow. If it will fool a fish without a live-bait dressing, imagine what it will do with the easy meal attached.

There are times of course when no amount of flipping and flashing will inspire a strike. So what's left? Add a little more realism. Again vertical fishing with the Rapala offers this advantage—more realism—whereas horizontal fishing (casting and trolling) is limited.

Walleyes are notoriously finicky, particularly in the winter. That means the usual jigging action, despite its realistic appearance, simply will not draw a strike. One day on Mille Lacs Lake, a famous walleye hotspot in Minnesota, the walleyes seemed to be bored with everything, including the Rapala. I had tried just about every jigging contortion possible under the circumstances. Still nothing worked.

Finally, I dropped the Rapala all the way to the bottom, let it pause briefly, then—with a sharp snap upwards—I brought the swimming lure upwards only to let it dead fall to the bottom again.

I repeated the action several times, carefully watching the line. Suddenly—what I thought was the lure hitting the bottom— the line stopped. The first walleye of the day was on. The fish must have inhaled the lure a mere inch or so from the bottom. I also learned later why that particular action suddenly worked. The weighted Rapala, hitting the soft bottom then being yanked upwards, was stirring light clouds of silt up off of the bottom. The appearance of the clouds apparently excited the walleyes or at least attracted their attention. Creating "smoke" by bottom-bouncing the Rapala may not always work but tuck the idea away. It may make the difference someday if you're fishing the right bottom-type.

One more thing about vertical fishing. Because it is an uncommon method of fishing artificial lures, there is a wilderness of techniques yet to be discovered. The known techniques do work as more fishermen will discover when they try. And as more anglers discover the satisfaction of fishing artificials and fooling fish— while being restricted to one plane, up and down,—more methods will be developed.

Of course, it's not a major restriction. If you think about it, fish can only be in one of two places. Up or down.

ART MORASKI

*Further evidence that we are truly living in a "break out" age of
knowledge about fish and sportfishing is offered by the findings of
a young angler-researcher from southeastern Wisconsin. For the
past six years, Art Moraski, 30, has been exhaustively investigat-
ing every dimension of night fishing.*

*Although greatly encouraged by his results to date, Art is the
first to admit the area of nocturnal angling is still a new frontier:
the "virgin territory" of modern sportfishing, as he puts it. He
feels, for instance, that a more complete understanding of the
predator-prey relationship in lakes without a significant forage
factor (typical of many of the "overfished" waters close to our
urban centers) is fundamental to a better understanding of fish
behavior and making better catches.*

*In the following story, he addresses that problem head-on and
offers some workable new concepts which seem destined to rank
with the findings of Buck Perry and other true pioneers.*

*Research Editor of "Man Vs. Muskie Digest" and field editor of
"Hook and Shell" magazine, Art is also author of the two books,
NIGHT FISHING, PART I, and, NIGHT FISHING, PART II. You
may write him at 3211 West Franklin Terrace*

Franklin, Wisconsin

53132

RAPALAS REVOLUTIONIZE NIGHT FISHING

I researched night fishing for six years. Researching night fishing entailed the task of finding out when fish moved, why they moved, and where they moved to. I kept this project entirely to myself because I knew I was onto something really big. I would *see* many big fish with my equipment in lakes right near my home. Lakes that have a great deal of fishing pressure. Lakes that you and I would have normally passed up without blinking an eyelash. I realized I was looking at a whole new ball game. At first I asked a lot of questions, and ironically *no* one had answers to them. So I had the idea that I was in this alone. I kept records of fish movements and conditions, and this was all in a fishing period in history where structure fishing was evolving. However, there were things happening at night that were contrary to daytime activities. Well, let's say that maybe these things were happening during the daytime, but we as fishermen were *not entirely* aware of them. For instance:

THE WEED WALLEYE

We have all caught walleyes in the weeds at some time or another, and generally we pass it off as being another one of those freak fish. I believe that, unless we were all researchers, we may have thought about it for a few minutes but probably disregarded the incidents and continued fishing in our own fashion.

In my research at night, I have found that walleyes will relate to weeds in certain types of lakes more so than others. In a lake where the weeds are common, and substantial numbers of predators are common, and where the lakes *lack* suspended populations of cisco, herring, shad, whitefish, alewives, brook silver-sides, etc., walleyes will consistently relate to weeds.

Many times their night movements will outnumber their

daytime movements. Fish are basically controlled by environmental conditions. Walleyes are the migratory fish of the central to northern parts of the country. I have kept a close watch on this species, the king of the dinner table. Under certain conditions, the walleye will move up very close to shore and onto the gravel bars to feed. *The very best condition is: the third day of any type of steady weather conditions. During this condition, walleyes are active and generally in a positive feeding mood. If the third day or night has a low pressure system dominating, this would be an even better condition.* Under these conditions, walleye will move into the food shelf and roam the areas near shore in search of easy prey . . . leeches . . . baitfish . . . salamanders . . . snakes . . . crayfish . . . and a countless number of others.

There are many ways to catch these very big fish, and some of the tactics I employ are mentioned here. When you are on a lake and darkness is approaching, DO NOT LEAVE. YOU WILL MISS MAJOR MIGRATIONS. THE NIGHT TIME IS THE RIGHT TIME. Under general conditions, meaning neither the best nor the worst, walleyes will move up from the deeper water (if you are on a lake that contains a suspended baitfish population) or will become active from within the weeds (if you are on the type lake that has abundant numbers of northern and muskie, but without suspended baitfish populations). In my books I classify these lakes, but for now we will just make mention of it. So on WEEDY LAKES WITH ABUNDANT NUMBERS OF NORTHERNS AND MUSKIE, BUT WITHOUT SUSPENDED POPULATIONS OF FORAGE, there are certain methods I apply. BEFORE YOU TRY THEM, MAKE SURE YOU UNDERSTAND YOUR STATE LAWS ABOUT BOATING AT NIGHT (or any other time). Walleyes will relate to cabbage, cabomba, and sand grass and occasionally reeds and rushes in the event that the major weeds are not available. When working the weeds for walleyes at night, you must first distinguish which type of weed you're working in. If your weed growth leaves a zone of water between the weed tops and the surface, use the following method.

1. At night, the walleyes will be in the shallows searching for food. You must be extremely quiet. If you are still or on a very

slow drift pattern and shallow, your lights make a lot of difference. If you are on a fast drift pattern or a troll, your lights will not interfere with your fishing success. For a slow drift pattern, cast from your boat toward shore. Toss a #9 Countdown Rapala in shallow and retrieve it back very slowly, twitching it every once in a while. Often you will notice a walleye following it right up to the boat. When you get a strike, set the hooks well, but don't overdo it. This is one of the reasons I use Rapalas; those Finlanders make sharp hooks! My own personal preference in colors is this: I always make sure I have silver ones with me—I use the gold in darker waters, blue in waters that contain trout and suspended populations of forage fish, and red in waters that contain carp and in good bassin' waters. Here's an example of Point 1.

The bulky design of the #9 Countdown Rapala gives it a good healthy minnow appearance. Fish must feel they're really getting a good meal on that #9 Countdown.

When largemouth bass are suspended in the weeds, I have found that using the above method worked very well on them.

Often times, the Rapala will just have hit the water and the bass will come up splashing with that bait, as though they were lying in wait for the cast!

2. If the weeds grow to the top of the water, try this: If you can find pockets in these weeds, you're in for a real treat. Some bass will practically live in the weeds, and at night they will suspend in these pockets. When they are there, all it takes is for a seemingly injured minnow to start flopping around on the surface near the pockets. The result is a nice stringer of hogs.

On lakes that have large predator factors and lack suspended baitfish, weed clumps are very excellent areas to fish at night. In the northern part of the country, bass migrate more on a vertical plane than on a long horizontal one, unless they are the principal predator in the lake. Many times bass will move a few feet higher in a weed bed and start to feed, rather than migrating from a different area. At night they usually suspend in the pockets or weed clumps. They will always be in proximity to their food. Crayfish are light-sensitive and are very active at night. Many aquatic insects are light-sensitive and are *only* active at night. In their mass vertical movement, baitfish follow the insects and, in turn,

are followed by suspended bass feeding on baitfish and crabs. Tossing a Rapala into these areas is very productive. I like to use the Deep-Diver 90 in this type of situation. Don't worry about going into the weeds occasionally. Many times when you dive the Deep-Diver 90, stop your retrieve for a split second and then resume cranking. A lot of times you'll get the hit on that split second stop. Other methods on weed clumps are twitching your bait on the surface, or a *very, very slow* retrieve. The Rapala is made so that even during your slowest retrieves your Rapala is working for you with natural, lifelike action.

If you are working a gravel slope for walleyes and it is early in the evening, position your boat in the shallow water, work your bait from the deep water back to the shallows. Later, after dark,

EARLY EVENING-
DEEP TO SHALLOW

position your boat in the deeper water and work your bait from the shallows to the deep. I like to use a #9 or #11 Countdown Rapala. Flip it out and let it settle.When your line indicates your Rapala is on the bottom, start a very slow jerking-and-settle type retrieve. Sometimes the take will be in mid-water, and it will seem that your bait has just stopped and did not sink all the way down. In this case, reel up the slack quickly, get a good eight o'clock position and set that hook!

On drift passes at night, work the shorelines which have the most available food. With two people in the boat, you can fan cast the shoreline and, in most cases, sections of the first break as you move on a 45 degree angle to the shore. The person working the

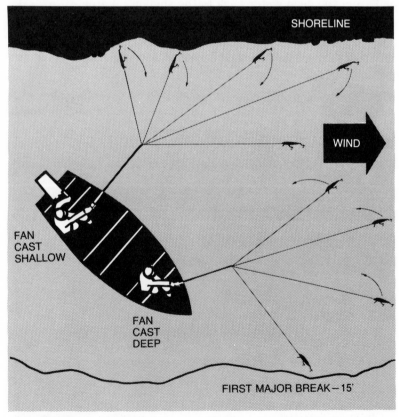

shore-side can, and should, use a floating Rapala. The floater can be worked in extremely shallow water, and is very effective because it looks like an injured minnow. Early in the evening, all of these areas can be worked with moderate to fast-moving Rapalas. As evening turns to darkness, slower retrieves produce much better. The guy who is working the outside should have one rod set up for a Deep-Diver on the first break, and a Countdown model for the water between.

Points of land and points of islands should never be passed up. One reason walleyes are easily caught in fyke nets is that they are "contour followers"—following the wall which leads them to the opening of the net, which they enter and become trapped. Many times at night walleyes are following the contours. Points and bars are natural gathering areas, purely from location aspects. When working these areas with your Rapalas, work them slowly. Slowly is a key word for several reasons: (1) Walleyes are generally casual feeders, not wanting to over-exert themselves in pursuit of a bait when they are in a negative or neutral feeding mood. (2) When walleyes are shallow, they are finicky and spook easily. You must use caution in retaining contact with the school.

In a trolling pattern, lights are not as much a negative factor as when you are casting for the shallow fish. When working shallow on a trolling pattern, I "long line" it, letting out up to 75 yards of line while trolling with my electric motor. All is slow and

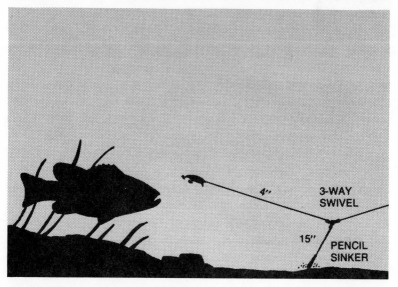

quiet, and I can concentrate all my efforts on fishing. In the shallow water areas, I use the floating Rapalas and work them slowly. In deeper waters, 12 to 18 feet, I use the Countdown Rapalas. In deep water, I use a floating Rapala with a sinker and three-way swivel. I have found this method to be one of the most successful ways to catch many species of fish at night. The sinker is called a Reb Pencil sinker.

MANY TIMES I AM ASKED, "WHAT ABOUT THE AVERAGE FISHERMAN WHO WANTS TO FISH AT NIGHT, BUT DOES NOT FEEL RIGHT DOING IT, OR DOES NOT HAVE THE TIME TO PURSUE IT?"

I sympathize with those questions. Many people would like to try fishing at night but just do not have enough confidence to begin. I truly understand the question and have an answer for it. But, first, let me state some very interesting points about night fishing:

1. When walleyes are moving into shallow water, they are very finicky and only the proper methods will take them. In a boat, you have to be extremely quiet and work very carefully.

2. Once the walleyes have moved into the shallows, which is pretty early by the clock in some lakes, you have a *BETTER* chance of catching them from *SHORE*. This means you don't have to take off work. If you are limited for time and cannot possibly rent a boat, you can still have a lot of fun catching walleyes. Here's what to do. Go to your favorite walleye lake and take about five Rapalas with you: two floaters, one Deep-Diver, and two Countdowns. The Deep-Diver is for those lakes with sharp shoreline breaks. At home, put a small split ring on each Rapala and tie an improved clinch knot on the split ring of the one you're going to try first. Now if you know any areas that have gravel bars that come right up to shore, go to those shorelines. At this stage of the game try to use little or no light. Walk very slowly up to the shoreline or on the pier. Cast out and reel fast for about 5 feet, then crank very slowly. If you are in a good walleye area and are using the Rapala in the fashion described, you will catch yourself some frying-pan fish! I do this many times in the course of the year, and catch a lot of fish doing it.

MUSKIE

Through my research, I have gotten into fishing for muskie at night. It is difficult. I have used Rapalas from the Magnum size to the small #9 Countdowns for this type of fishing. I like to use a floater over weed beds (preferably cabbage) and just shake the heck out of the bait. When a muskie takes it, your heart just has to go 100 miles an hour! I bet you wonder if a muskie can see at night. Here is an excerpt taken from one of my books on night fishing:

NIGHT FISHING PART 1 . . . PAGE 14 & 15 . . . by ART MORASKI

CAN MUSKIES SEE AT NIGHT? DO THEY FEED AT NIGHT?

Little Green Lake, Green Lake, Co., Wisconsin. The night was pitch black, a low pressure system was dominant. The southern side of the lake produces real good walleyes and I have seen muskie here. So here I am, in the middle of the night, going muskie fishing. Gale Radtke of Radtke's Landing says, "Come on, let's go for a beer and a bite to eat." I had to refuse him. I was hot on this muskie kick and was working for my eighth one in eight days. (That's eight legals in eight days.) Well, doggone! I tried everything. I put that ole' Rapala to work and tried every type of retrieve I could think of. Now I knew that muskie roamed in and out of this area all of the time. Then I tried something a little different. I cranked that 5-to-1 retrieve as fast as I could go in one direction without fouling up. I did this for about five minutes, then WHAMMMMMMMMMM out of the water it came! I had one! What a ball! Walleyes sure don't jump like that! All over the place, around the boat, and finally in the net. This muskie had that #9 silver Rapala ALL THE WAY DOWN HIS THROAT! Now this is a pitch-black night, and I was cranking that 5-to-1 retrieve as fast as my hand could possibly go in one direction.

Following is what a school of muskies looks like. If you get into them you will need a good supply of Rapalas because they *can* be caught. Muskies will roam around the weed beds, and occasionally just lie there suspended above the weeds. Throughout fishing history, there have been many documented stories about catching huge, huge muskies at night. Night fishing is a whole new ball

game. I have researched this ball game deeply, and I know that those who pursue it will get fish in sizes they never thought possible.

During my winter activities, I spend a lot of time fishing near warm water discharges into Lake Michigan. Some fish are ripe with spawn prematurely due to the warm water discharges long before the males are in. At night we catch many big German browns using spawn-sacks, minnows, and Rapalas. All of these things are happening at night, and the majority of the fishermen are not even aware of it. Those are the times when you do not have to rent or own a boat, and still catch really decent fish. All that you really need is a few Rapalas, a decent rod and reel, warm clothing, your lunch pail and a stringer to bring home your fish.

*The Original Floating Rapala, "The Lure Fish Can't Pass Up," revolution-
ized sportfishing by introducing balsa wood technology. Each model,
ranging in length from 2 to 7 inches, represents over 30 painstaking
production steps. Each Rapala is individually hand tank-tested and
adjusted to assure most lifelike swimming action ever attained in an
artificial lure. Colors are silver, perch, gold, blue and fluorescent red.*

Countdown Rapalas, from 2 to 4 3/8 inches in length, are weighted to sink at a uniform rate and retrieve at any speed with the same inimitable, lifelike swimming action as the Original Floating model. The Countdown Rapala comes in silver, perch, gold, blue and fluorescent red. Each lure is individually tank-tested and carefully balanced to the highest Rapala standards.

The Jointed Floating Rapala is the latest addition to the world-famous line of handcrafted fishing lures. Its distinguishing characteristic is a livlier, attention-getting action at a slower rate of retrieve. Like all Rapalas, each of the new jointed models is hand tank-tested and balanced. Jointed Floating Rapalas come in three sizes, 2 3/4 to 4 3/8 inches, and in the four familiar Rapala colors: silver, gold, blue and fluorescent red.

The world's finest crank bait because it's based on the precision balsa wood technology pioneered by Laurie Rapala. Perfectly balanced via individual tank-testing, each Fat Rap runs true at slow or fast speeds. A floating lure that dives when retrieved, the long nose fends off underwater obstacles and lure surfaces upon any pause. Needle-sharp hooks hook the most cautious sport fish: a superb tool for cranking lunkers up out of intermediate depths and heavy cover. Comes in two sizes, 2 inches, 3/8 oz., and 2 3/4 inches, 1/2 oz. Colors are crawdad, shad, perch and fluorescent red.

The Magnum Floating and Sinking Rapalas are extra big and strong for heavyweight, trophy fish; both fresh and saltwater. Magnums have corrosion-resistant hooks, heavy-duty lips and bodies for easier casting and anti-broaching, even when trolled at higher speeds in rough salt water. Magnum Floating and Sinking Rapalas come in two sizes, 5 1/4 and 7- inch lengths, and five colors: silver, gold, blue, fluorescent red and the new silver mackerel color.

Jigging Action Rapalas give a new vertical dimension to both summer and winter fishing. The Rapala Balanced and Pilkki Jigging Lures reach fish unattainable through other methods. The Balanced Model (above) comes in four sizes, 1½ to 3½ inches in length, and in three colors.

The Pilkki Model (below) is available in two sizes, 1⅜ and 2¼ inches, and six colors: nickel red, nickel black, copper red, copper black, brass red and brass black. The Balanced Model moves faster and covers a wider area. The Pilkki Model feature a slow, fluttering action. The two lures attract all types of gamefish.

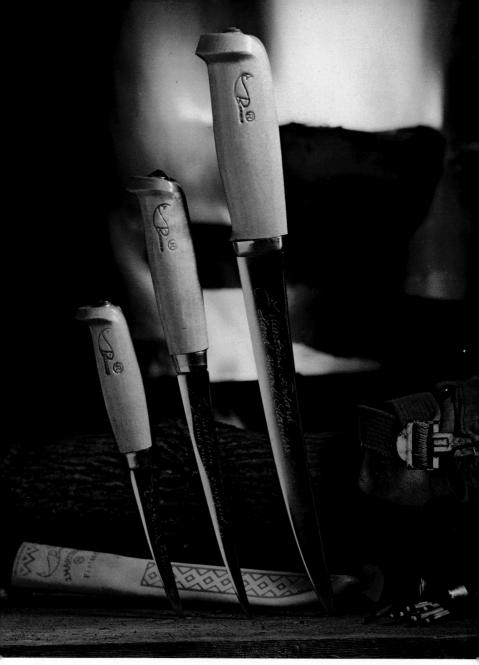

Functional Scandanavian beauty marks all three Rapala "Fish 'N Fillet" knives, which are seen worldwide in more fishing camps and on more charter boats than any other. Curved, flexible Swedish stainless steel blades are custom-ground to stay razor-sharp through the hardest use, yet can be honed by hand. Blade lengths are 4,6 and 9 inches. Each comes in distinctive Laplander tooled leather sheath.

Normark knives are the serious outdoorsman's selection for the ultimate in utility and beauty. Fine hand craftsmanship is apparent in the Normark Presentation Hunting Knife and Filleting Knife and the folding Presentation Little Swede and Big Swede game and utility knives. The latter feature lanyard loops and lanyards; the Hunting and Filleting knives come in tooled oxhide leather sheaths.

JACK MACIOSEK

There is probably no better walleye fisherman in the entire state of Minnesota than Jack Maciosek. That is a risky, even reckless, statement because the walleye is Minnesota's state fish and, annually, hundreds of thousands of natives seek out this table favorite, each convinced that he or she can fool walleyes when all others fail. But Jack never seems to fail and his full strings usually contain an eye-popper or two; bronze giants in the eight, nine and even ten pound range!

Maciosek operates Jack's Twin Bay resort, near the town of Isle, on Lake Mille Lacs, a shallow, 20-mile-in-diameter dish which, some are convinced, is God's own walleye factory. This would seem to give Jack a distinct advantage and he is a peerless angler and boat operator. He has been the subject of several stories on his specialty in national magazines and he is the co-sponsor of a big annual walleye tournament on his lake. Because Jack is an affable, generous man, he shared his Rapala walleye fishing secrets with us.

TAKING BIG WALLEYES AT NIGHT

The first time I saw the Rapala in action was on a muskie trip to Canada with Ray Ostrom. He said, "I've got a new bait I want you to try." I replied, okay, that it was my first muskie trip, anyway, and that one muskie bait must be as good as another because no one *ever* caught one of those monsters until after they'd been fishing them for five or ten years, at least.

But the joke was on me! I caught three keeper muskies that day, the biggest 35 pounds (releasing all but the trophy, which is now on my wall) on a #18 floating gold Rapala. Needless to say, I became an instant believer and begged a couple of the smaller models to take back to my resort so I could try them on Mille Lacs.

Until that day, I'd fished Mille Lacs for 20 years. Like other experienced anglers, I took most of my walleyes at night, usually by trolling one of the "banana" baits dressed out with nightcrawlers. Somehow, though, this always disturbed me. The technique involved trolling through shallow waters. I knew that this was the walleyes' night-time habitat and that the outboard motor was bound to spook the biggest and the wariest of these fish.

So by trial and error, I slowly evolved the perfect technique for catching lots of big walleyes at night on the reefs and bars that ring most of Mille Lacs. This approach is very effective until, normally, early July, when warming water temperatures disperse the schooling walleyes and they seek out the mud flats in the middle of the lake.

One picture is worth a million words. As the sketch indicates, I approach a known walleye reef *very quietly*, just about nightfall. And I'm even more quiet when I drop the anchor (try not to make a sound!!) *upwind* of and within casting distance of the *crown of the reef*. Before it gets dark, I rig my spincasting outfit with a #9 Rapala (the model of which I'll explain in a moment), tying the lure directly to the 10 pound test mono line. If it is a calm or relatively windless night, I select the #9 *Countdown* model and cast it *beyond* the crown of the reef, into the deeper water on the far side from my boat. When fishing this way, keep your rod tip up and make your retrieve "slow and high", swimming the lure directly over the shallowest part of the rocks. When it is in deeper water, closer to the boat, you can drop the tip again and deepen the retrieve. Also, "fan cast" the reef, working both sides in addition to the crown. Walleyes, when they come in schools, will be working all around the reef.

On a *windy* evening, use the #9 gold original *floating* Rapala because there is more of a chance of getting hung up when the top of the reef is awash in a brisk breeze. However, the fishing action is invariably better on a windy night. I am of the opinion that the wave action around the boulders and rocks of the bar tends to dislodge minnows and crayfish seeking refuge there. This brings the big walleyes out in numbers. They actually seem to hunt in "wolfpacks" — attacking in waves to smash any kind of forage.

The Rapala has it head and shoulders over all lures here because of its lightness, ease of retrieve and ability to fool this usually very wary fish. One important tip: when immense Mille Lacs walleyes are night-feeding on a wind-blown reef, they hit like there's no tomorrow! Many (and I mean many!) experienced fishermen have been shocked by the savagery of their attack. Some have actually lost rods and reels! So hold tight, and be ready to battle back!

Knowledge of the reefs is important. It can be gained with experience. The important thing is to anchor (and, again, you can't be too quiet!) on the upwind side of the reef, close enough to permit a cast *beyond* the peak, which may be only a foot or two under water. Many of the bars are so small that you need to anchor only once to give them a good working over. But a long, narrow bar should be worked from several different anchorages; each one of which will put a new stretch of rocks under attack.

Next to the sound of a running motor, the thing that spooks

our night-feeding walleyes most is any kind of light falling on the water. We carry a dim lantern to re-tie knots and disengage hooks; but always keep it on the very bottom of the boat. Even a faint glimmer on the water can put the walleyes off the bar for minutes; or perhaps for the entire night!

We've also discovered that a stretchable, rubber landing net is ideal for this kind of fishing. It minimizes hang-ups which are so common in the mesh of conventional nylon nets. And because it's flat, we often use the unextended rubber net as a paddle to actually "scoop" the fish into the boat. When they are coming in waves, it's often better to scoop than to risk a time-consuming (and highly frustrating) hook-up in the nylon!

There's no better way to fish for big walleyes than on Lake Mille Lacs on a windy evening. I hope that some of these techniques will work on your favorite walleye lake. But wherever, or however, you fish for walleyes, there is no better lure (day or night) than the Rapala.

Editors' Note: Jack Maciosek's walleye-whomping tips were seconded heartily in a recent conversation with Price Taylor, famous Canadian resorter and walleye guide who records startling catches where the Moon River enters Georgian Bay in south-western Ontario.

Price makes an additional, valid point. He always uses an improved clinch knot when tying his monofilament line directly to the eye of the Rapala. He adds: *when securing your knot, be*

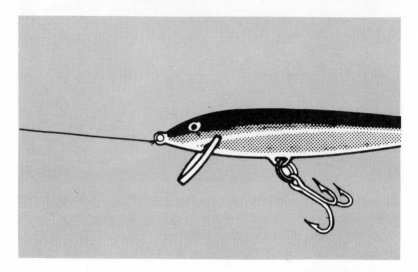

sure to keep it in the lower 30 degrees of the arc inscribed by the eye of the lure. This way, he says, the lure will trail properly when trolled or cast at night; when it is literally impossible to visually check the action of the Rapala. But with a low tie-off, says Price Taylor, you can be comfortably assured that the Rapala is swimming with the exaggerated action so effective on a slow retrieve — constantly ready to fool one of those voracious, night-feeding walleyes.

JOHN SIEGEL

A veteran trophy angler for all varieties of gamefish, John Siegel, to the knowledge of the editors, has probably caught more lake trout between 30 and 50 pounds than any other person. John is a Minneapolis heating and air condition engineer-contractor who loves to ventilate his lungs in the crystal-clear air of Chantrey Inlet, Lake Tazin and, particularly, Great Bear Lake: the world's largest mass of fresh cold water and the home of its very largest lake trout.

His biggest trophy from Great Bear is a 52-pounder, but John has caught and released countless Arctic lakers in the 30- and 40-pound class. In the following article, John generously offered to share the secrets of his lake trout fishing success.

MONSTER LAKE TROUT

I began fishing lake trout in Canada about 35 years ago, reaching Great Bear Lake, even then the last frontier, in 1955. Its lunker trout were an immediate revelation! I had fished salt water from Yucatan to the Outer Banks, from the Baja Peninsula to the Pacific Northwest, and for all of our freshwater gamefish. But to me, no fish fights exactly like a laker and the majesty of Great Bear must be experienced to be believed.

First of all, it's a truly immense lake; more than 1,200 square miles of surface area and almost 1,700 miles of shore line. The water is gin-clear and most of the lake remains unbelievably cold during the short angling season, which runs only from mid-summer to early fall. However, the weather is usually splendid during the season with little rain and tolerable air temperatures, if you bring the proper clothing. With modern jet air transportation, Great Bear is less than a day's flight from cities like Chicago and Minneapolis, with transfer to the several fly-in camps at Yellowknife, N.W.T.

In fishing Great Bear, my friends accuse me of being a fanatic on one subject, and perhaps I am, because it is so paramount. *Water temperature is all important. Like all lake trout, those of Great Bear have a preferred temperature range. Theirs is between 46 and 51 degrees F. Find that range of water temperature and you will soon be on your way to some big lake trout.* This does not mean that smaller trout will not frequent warmer water. But if you are looking for a Great Bear trophy, it would be a rarity to find him in any other temperature range.

I consider this factor so important that a water temperature gauge is a necessity on Great Bear. It is even more important than an electronic depth finder! In fact, I always carry two on my trips up there, in case one fails or is lost. The cost is minimal, compared to the total investment, and the benefits are almost immeasurable because the temperature probe multiples your fishing effectiveness many times over. The gauge keeps you away from unproductive water, and it's a mighty big lake!

We know pretty well where to begin to look for that 46 to 51 degree water. Because of the short season (the camps are open only from late June to September!) the main lake is often completely iced up until the second or third week of July. Early on, when the main lake is out, because of ice; we then go *way* up into the bays—to the very mouths of entering streams and rivers, where the inflowing water is the warmest.

There, early in the short season, we find optimal temperature ranges in two, three or four feet of water. I've seen deep-bellied lakers with their dorsal fins just breaking water as they seek out their temperature. As the season progresses, the remainder of the bay will warm up, so we move out; always probing the water for that ideal temperature range. For me, the best times on Great Bear have been when the big bays are fully open but the main lake is still under ice. That's usually the case about the middle of July. Water in the main lake, by the way, seldom gets much warmer than 39 degrees F! (Of course, this doesn't mean that there are no trout in the main lake. Test nettings have yielded lakers from as deep as 1,300 feet. But for the best fishing, work the bays.)

Once we've found a promising area of 46 to 51 degree water, we begin angling. As we do, we are always mindful of a strange, perhaps unscientific, fact; but one that thus far has always held true and is of great assistance to us in locating large, trophy trout; or eliminating waters that hold only smaller (for Great Bear Lake) specimens.

That fact is this: the lake trout of Great Bear Lake seem to carry three distinct colorations: silver (or white), bronze and what we call "redfin" because of a definite rosy hue to the tails and larger fins. *The really monster lakers are all silver or white in color. We seek out populations of these fish in quest of the trophies.* When we encounter trout with darker, bronze backs or the "redfin" variety, we move on in search of their lighter-hued cousins. Again, I know of no genetic or environmental explanation for this occurrence; it's just one of those facts of fishing life which invariably works. In addition to these two elements—the ideal temperature range and the "white" subspecie of trout—when we find a third—*a hard, clay bottom*—then we have conditions that make for ideal trophy angling.

Once on the track of the big silver-sides, we either cast or troll: trolling if the depth is ten feet or more, casting in shallower water. In either case, I begin with a Rapala tied directly to my monofilament line with a "Uni" or loop-knot of some kind: 15-pound test line on the casting rig, 20-pound test on the trolling outfit. Like many other veteran Rapala users, I'm convinced that unnecessary terminal tackle (snaps, rings, swivels, etc.) only compounds the chance of tackle failure and restricts the action of the lure. It is true that lake trout have teeth, but neither as many nor as large as some other gamefish. Lake trout do not pose a big cut-off problem.

Casting, or at the shallowest trolling level (ten feet), I'll use the #18 seven-inch *floating* Rapala, either the original standard model or the Magnum. At the next deepest level (ten to 15 feet), I go to the Countdown in the larger #18 Magnum size. In 15 feet of water or over, my choice is to troll the regular #18 floater

with a three-way swivel and enough weight to bump the bottom with the sinker as I pump the rig with my rod tip. I strongly suggest that while trolling you follow the same procedure: pump the tip of your rod, making the Rapala speed up and slow down while the sinker bumps bottom, preferably a clay surface.

Casting on Great Bear is largely a matter of "jump" fishing, which beats trolling all hollow when it comes to fun and excitement. The water is so fantastically clear that you can see down many feet. (One of the early explorers was able to spot a white cloth submerged to more than 100 feet!) So, when you're trolling and come into a nice school of trout, you pick up your lines and go to the casting outfits. Casting those clear water reefs allows you to see the follow. It's not only a great thrill but it also lets you take your lure away from the smaller fish so you won't have to unhook them.

Color-wise, the lakers of Great Bear seem to have no great preference; although, like so many trout, they often will go for the flourescent red Rapalas when all else seems to fail. However, they'll usually offer freely at any of the colors. Color, like trolling speed, is a matter of experimentation. We never troll excessively fast or slow. We test only variations within the usual trolling range. When trolling I prefer an "S" pattern. This allows you more coverage and you'll spook fewer fish in the path of the boat in this gin-clear water.

Rod-type is very important in this kind of fishing. I use relatively light rods for both trolling and casting, five to six feet in length. But I have discovered that the "double taper" or "parabolic" construction is tops for these big trout. That's the kind of rod with a light, sensitive tip, but a stout mid-section which translates the tip-action to the butt. This permits me to keep heavy pressure on the fish while the tip remains relatively unstressed; or at least lively enough to respond when the hooked trout decides to surface.

And make no mistake: *that moment of surfacing is vital because of the way the trout of Great Bear fight.* When initially hooked, they make the habitual strong run, usually sounding as they go. After setting the hook, vigorously but not violently, I begin to pump the trout, attempting to gain line, with the drag on my Quick bait casting reel set fairly high: to within one or two pounds of the breaking strength of the line.

But when the trout decides to surface, as he inevitably will, *you've got to be ready to do two things, and do them right now!!*

1. *Loosen the star drag,* reducing some of the tension on the line, and,
2. *Let your rod tip come into full play,* so the trout does not sense any absolute resistance that would permit him to get away with a "no no."

The "no no" consists of his very rapidly and skillfully rolling himself up in your line on the surface.

The results of this sequence are invariably catastrophic. A truly large Great Bear trout is so strong that when snubbed by the main tackle, he will roll up in your line like a flywheel gone crazy and out of control! With his tremendous leverage and sharp gill covers, he can easily tear out the hooks or cut the line. I salvaged a big spoon that a 45-pound trout actually bent with his jaws when he gained some leverage in the bottom of the boat! So the rule is: *"fight them down":* be generous to a surfacing fish. Give him immediate reduced drag and the pliant tip of your rod so he doesn't tear up your terminal tackle.

When fighting a large trout, be on the lookout for a discharge of large bubbles. It portends a surfacing fish. Stand by to loosen the drag and elevate your tip. If you do this, the fish will sound. Then you again *tighten* the drag and pump him up. You'll be repeating this loosening-tightening-loosening procedure many times over with a big trout. It took me more than one hour and 45 minutes to land my 52 pound fish. I don't know how many times he surfaced. But I *do* know that he never had a chance to roll up in the line. Otherwise, it would have been goodbye trout!

That 52-pounder was also instructive in that I hooked and landed him in only three or four feet of water, just off the mouth of a stream, deep inside a bay. We knew that it was a good spot because the stream had washed some organic material onto the lake bed over which the trout were feeding. I cast a #18 silver floating Rapala in toward shore and caused it to walk back through the clay and muck, kicking up little clouds or puffs as it came. This must have attracted the trout. You could see the immense swirl on the surface when he hit. It was a top fishing thrill.

We also emphasize fish release at Great Bear because the waters there are so cold and sterile, nutritionally, that it takes a lake trout 14 years to mature: to even begin spawning!! Moreover, the mature fish, as individuals, spawn only every second or third year, and gain less than a pound a year during their early, critical growth period. (My 52-pounder must have been close to 45 years old!!) So the rule at Great Bear is: keep only eating fish and a trophy; releasing other trophies and those in the "younger" age classes (really, 20 to 30 years old!) upon whose spawning the future of this great sports fishery depends.

In his excellent fish release chapter in this book, Buck Rogers tells the correct way to free a fish from the hooks (even cutting them off, if this is necessary) and how to "pump" the returned fish—moving it gently fore-and-aft in the hands so oxygen-rich water at the surface is moved over the gills. We keep pumping until the fish is strong enough to swim away under its own power, which invariably happens when you use the correct technique. Occasionally it has been necessary to spend more than an hour working with a large trout until it has regained sufficient oxygen to be released.

Our observations have taught us that the lake herring is the main forage of the Great Bear trout. I feel that is why the Rapala is so uniquely effective in this and many other waters; not only because of its uncanny resemblance to the lake herring, but because of its swimming, rolling lifelike action which causes trout to sometimes prefer it over the real thing.

This was driven home to me on a fly-in trip to Chantrey Inlet, to fish for lakers in the fast-flowing rivers which enter the Arctic Ocean there. I found that the sinking Magnum Rapala works well if it is slowly let down from your feet into the turbulent channels and runs. I've seen big trout recklessly charge out from their sanctuaries behind sheltering rocks to nail the big Magnum as it quivvers in the current like a stricken forage fish.

First-timers to Great Bear are urged to bring warm clothing, especially insulated underwear and a down-filled jacket, and their rain gear, although it is a naturally arid climate. Insects are not a problem on the big bays, but they can be annoying close to shore.

So I routinely bring an insect-net for my hat and some good bug repellent.

There are at least five or six good fishing camps on Great Bear strung out along its vast east-to-west orientation. I've come to the firm conviction that the largest fish are to be found on the east end. Recently, we have been staying at Arctic Circle Lodge; where accommodations, guides, boats, and motors are all excellent.

Wherever you go on Great Bear, I hope that you can utilize some of the know-how I have shared in this interview. If you do, I'm sure that you'll have an excellent chance of bringing back a trophy trout. I know that the Rapala method has greatly enhanced my success over the years at Great Bear Lake.

STU APTE

Stu Apte is a master angler who has fished the South Florida area since his boyhood days in Miami. Once one of the most sought after fishing guides in the Keys, and now a Pan American Airways Captain, he uses his off time to follow his fishing passion all over the world. He has done many network television specials for ABC's American Sportsman, including the original television pilot; Fishing for Big Tarpon in the Florida Keys. Stu is holder of more than 20 world records on light tackle, including his 154 lb. giant tarpon on a fly rod with 12 lb. test tippet.

Author of a number of articles and a recent book on light tackle techniques, "Stu Apte's Fishing in the Florida Keys", published by Windward Publishing, P.O. Box 370233, Miami, Fla. 33137. Apte is known as a "hard" fisherman who is on the water early and late in fair weather and foul, seeking the biggest fish on the lightest tackle.

A hard taskmaster, Stu goes out to win, and makes sure his tackle will do all he wants it to. If a change is indicated, he developes it, and is responsible for a number of innovations in the fishing world today.

TAKING GIANT TARPON

You can take big tarpon on the Rapala by plug casting or trolling almost anywhere in the cuts and bights of the Florida Keys, in the "mullet-muds," around the passes, and in deep bays like Miami's Government Cut, or Key West Harbor, primarily at night. Even shallower water, if it has good current, can hold giant tarpon, year 'round, but in great abundance in April, May and June.

One of the finest nights of tarpon fishing I ever had was about thirty miles from Key West, on the Gulf side of Bahia Honda Bridge in the Florida Keys. Conditions were perfect . . . . . a big moon, a clear night, the tide had just started out toward the Atlantic side of the bridge. I was fishing with Captain Lee Baker, a good friend and well-known guide, and we had just turned off the engine and begun drifting. All around us tarpon were rolling, and occasionally one would thrash the water, busting shrimp or mullet.

I started casting a blue and silver magnum Rapala, a Count-down 18. The water there was about 15 feet deep, so I cast out blind and let the lure sink, varying my rod tip on the retrieve. After the second cast I had reeled the lure most of the way in, it was now coming to the surface, wiggling and shimmying like a mullet about to jump. I felt a light tap, and as I hauled back on it two or three times to set the hook, a big, gill-rattling silver king burst out of the water, my lure dangling from its jaws. Keys' tarpon weigh in big, and this was a heavyweight! After a twenty minute battle, it lay exhausted at the gunwhale. Lee lip-gaffed it while I took back my Rapala, and we released the big fighter to thrill some other angler.

That fish was only the beginning. From there it was all "go."

For several hours I had a tarpon on almost every other cast. It was a super night. We decided to experiment with lures to see if the tarpon would grab everything. I tried four different types including bucktails, with and without worms, and another swimming lure, and I never got a single tap.

I went back to the Rapala and, bam, felt a hit. At times, even the giant tarpon only gives a light bump when it strikes. No crashing jolt as you might expect with a fish that size, but when it realizes it's hooked, the fireworks start. There is nothing like the awesome silver king when it comes to sheer power and frightening aerobatics. After that night, I never go into the Key's "back country" without a tackle box full of Rapalas.

When trolling in Key West Harbor, bend the Rapala's metal lip to bring the lure closer to the bottom, where the big tarpon are lying, as deep as thirty feet. Sometimes they will stack up on the edge of the main channel in twenty feet of water, or even less. It is best to troll the Rapala very slowly, letting it sink, with just enough speed to keep it moving, and hold the rod tip low to have plenty of room for setting the hook. Coming in from behind, towards the boat, a tarpon doesn't hit hard enough to pull the rod down. When there is a stop, or tap, set the hook with three or four backward jerks.

Plug casting, spinning, or trolling, I use standard gear with 15 lb. test line, rigged with a Bimini twist knot to make two or three

---

ALBRIGHT KNOT

Used to connect lines of different diameters.

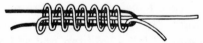

1. Double up the heavier line forming a long U. Take the lighter line up into the U, making approximately ten wraps towards the bottom of the U and around the U and the standing part of the lighter line. Bring the end of the lighter line out through the bottom of the U.

2. Tighten the knot by pulling slowly and evenly.

inches of double line coming off the 15 pounds and use an Albright knot to tie onto 30 pound test mono shock leader. I use about five or six feet of that, and tie a blood knot to connect the 30 pound with 15 to 20 inches of 80 pound test mono leader.

Connecting to the Rapala, I tie a form of loop knot in the 80 pound mono. There are a couple of different kinds, and one is called the "Parismina" loop, which I learned from a local guide down in Parismina, Costa Rica. It's like a "Perfection" loop, but attached to the lure. The other is a Nail Knot Loop.

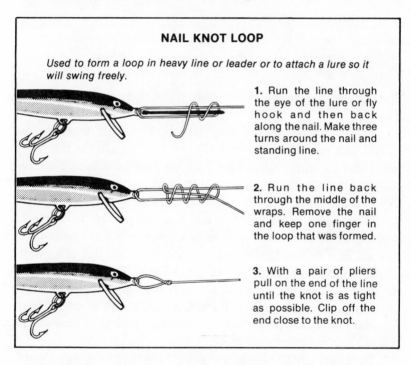

NAIL KNOT LOOP

Used to form a loop in heavy line or leader or to attach a lure so it will swing freely.

1. Run the line through the eye of the lure or fly hook and then back along the nail. Make three turns around the nail and standing line.

2. Run the line back through the middle of the wraps. Remove the nail and keep one finger in the loop that was formed.

3. With a pair of pliers pull on the end of the line until the knot is as tight as possible. Clip off the end close to the knot.

Fishing in Costa Rica, where the tarpon range from about 60 to 110 pounds, I use the orange and yellow Rapala, the Countdown 13. It's all daytime fishing and the water is not as deep, hardly more than 15 feet. I watch for the tarpon to roll, or follow a line of bubbles which indicates where a school of tarpon are moving.

The cast is made in front of the line of bubbles, far enough to let the lure sink towards the bottom. Sometimes I stick the rod tip down in the water to get more depth on the retrieve right away.

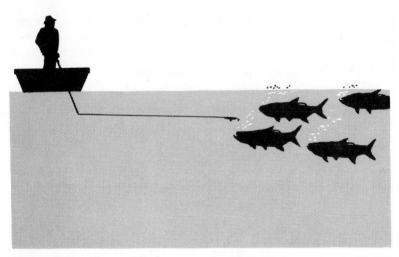

The biggest tarpon I've ever caught down there was on a Count-down 13.

There had been some very large fish moving through the passes, but not biting, when I tied on the Rapala. On the third cast I had a stop. By reflex I set the hook, bam, bam, bam. Nothing happened! I thought I had hooked the bottom, so I reeled up tight to jerk it loose, and it started moving out, slowly. Maybe a big jew-fish, I thought. Then up it came, heaving out of the surface, shaking its head. It was big, a huge tarpon over a 115 pounds. It jumped four or five times, slashing tons of water out of its way.

The fight was short, but very aerobatic. The tarpon doesn't struggle as long with the Rapala as it does on a smaller, single hook fly. It knows, I suppose, it has a mouthful. We lip-gaffed that one and found that, even with the violent shaking, one hook was still holding, behind the gill plate.

To make sure the hooks are going to perform the way I want them to, I use a pocket stone to hone them to an even finer point than the manufacturer. I file away, triangulating the point until it is so sharp it will dig into a thumbnail with no effort.

Pequari Lagoon in Costa Rica, is maybe two miles long and a quarter mile wide, but it's shallow to a depth of about four feet in the center. The tarpon like to lie along the channels sides, or on the bottom, and move very slowly, rolling, and burping their lines of bubbles.

I never run the engine in the area I intend to fish. Particularly in remote waters without much traffic as the combustion disturbs the tarpon—these armored giants are very sensitive—and though the noise may make them roll, they won't bite.

The lure action I use in Cost Rica varies a little from what I do in the Keys. After every two or three turns of the crank I give it a little double twitch, crank a few more times, and twitch it some more. That makes the lure dart, and really excites the fish even when they are not feeding. I've had fish follow the lure all the way to the transom, and right at leader length, stick their heads out, thinking their snack was getting away, and drench me with water as they struck.

Sometimes, going back over an area to cast again, my wife, Bernice, will troll the Countdown 13 Rapala, maybe 150 feet back, and we've caught an awful lot of tarpon that way too.

I think the Rapala looks like a mullet to the tarpon, and that's one of their favorite foods. I don't know what the color may mean to them, but they do want different colors at different times. I use every pattern. The main thing is to get the lures down where they are, and move it slowly, like a mullet wiggling along.

The floating Rapala works well casting around the shallower areas where a sinking lure may snag. Around the bays and bights, five to eight feet deep, the tarpon cruise the mullet-muds, feeding on the vast schools of mullet. Sometimes they skyrocket out of the water, when crashing into the baitfish.

The technique there is to ease the boat near a mullet-mud and anchor it, or stake it, and cast the floating Rapala all the way to the other side of the area, if you can, or into it, and work it back through. The tarpon will hammer it, and I've found, paradoxically, more success with the Rapala in this situation than with live mullet.

It's easier to cover the area, for one thing, and you can vary the depth of your lure, bringing it past many more fish, and getting more chances than with a live, swimming mullet.

In general, I like artificials better than live bait, and with giant tarpon, there is a Rapala for every situation of plug casting, trolling, and spinning. I wouldn't dream of going fishing without them.

OMRI THOMAS

Omri Thomas was born March 10, 1933, under Pisces, the sign of the fishes, and he has been angling ever since. A self-proclaimed absolute fishing nut, Omri has always been close to the water. He started life working in the merchant navy (trained by the Norwegians) and later served with the Austrailian Whaling Commission as a flenser: the hearty who strips a dead whale of its blubber.

After being wounded in Korea as a volunteer with the First Batallion of the Australian Regiment, Omri returned to England where he commenced a long career in the fishing tackle industry, starting as a professional flytier. A fishing and casting instructor, tournament caster and member of the British Casting Association, Omri says he is also proud to be managing director of Normark Sport Ltd. of Great Britain. As the following story illustrates, he is also an expert angler for two of the finest coldwater fish of northern Europe.

THE ATLANTIC SALMON AND SEA TROUT

To us in Europe, the Atlantic salmon justly deserves the title, "King of the Fresh Water." His domain embraces the northern half of the Atlantic Ocean, from Cape Cod along the North American shores and then across to Europe, from the island countries and Russia south into Spain.

I do much of my salmon fishing in Scotland where the fish is so common that one booster type was known to say, "There are more salmon rivers in Scotland than salmon caught in England." I assure you, that is an exaggeration. But salmon can be fished for all over Scotland and in every month of the year. Besides the British Isles, the Scandanavian countries, France, Spain, Portugal and Iceland also offer excellent angling for the species.

All Atlantic salmon, with few exceptions, return to their parent river for spawning, which occurs two or three times in the lives of most fish. The very largest fish, which have spent five or six years in the ocean (probably in a common feeding ground off Greenland) weigh up to 45 pounds when they return. There are isolated heavier fish, of course, and the heaviest tackle-caught Atlantic salmon weighed in at 79½ pounds when it was reeled from a Norwegian River. Recapture records indicate that salmon return 1,500 miles from the feeding grounds to spawn in their parent rivers, drawn there (according to current operative theories) by an accute sense of smell. Whatever the reason, the Atlantic salmon possesses one of nature's finest homing mechanisms.

Encyclopedist Al McClane has called the Atlantic species the "decathlon salmon," a happy term that indicates its ability to run, leap, struggle and summon seemingly hidden sources of energy: giving the angler lucky enough to hook one a combination of the fighting characteristics found in a half-dozen of the other great gamefish.

THE SALMON LIE

Salmon are completely unlike trout in their selection of temporary holding stations as they move up-river to spawn. From the eyes of an experienced trout fisherman, some of the most unlikely looking stretches of a stream might seem a perfect interim abode to the moving salmon. For instance, a confident trout angler, but a novice when it comes to salmon, might wade directly through a shallows, certain parts of which might constitute a lie for a "taking" fish.

The lesson is that much of the "picture" water we usually associate with cold water fish is, for some reason, completely unacceptable to the Atlantic salmon. Hundreds of yards of salmon-less water may flow beautifully between salmon lies. Some pools are only resting places, not "taking" lies, where the holding fish will steadfastly ignore even the most skillfully presented Rapala. With the advent of summer and falling water levels, salmon change their positions, apparently because of some difference of the flow of the stream. Unlike trout, salmon are not conscious of "feeding lanes."

My experience leads me to believe that in addition to certain well-known "taking" pools, the lies where Atlantic salmon are most likely to be found are fairly shallow, certainly not over five feet in depth. Salmon seek out these same lies and pools year after year. The novice salmon fisherman could waste precious hours (and money) seeking out these lies. He should certainly obtain the service of an experienced guide or the advice of knowledgeable local anglers. Blind casting is definitely not advised in seeking out the Atlantic salmon.

CHOOSING RAPALAS FOR ATLANTIC SALMON

Rapalas play an important part in the salmon fisherman's arsenal and accounts for some astonishing catches of this 'king of the fresh water'. There is a size and colour to suit all types of water and conditions the angler will meet. There are some rule of thumb methods of selection, namely, in low clear water size 5-7; normal water height, 9-11; and in high water and spates, size 13-18.

A lot depends on the size of the river. Larger rivers require larger baits, small rivers small baits. We find in Scotland, in spring, on the large rivers Magnums are called for. Regarding colour selection; in clear water a silver or blue/silver Rapala seems to kill better and in slightly brackish and coloured water the choice is gold or gold fluorescent red. In very slow flowing rivers Jointed Rapalas give that little more action. Water temperature plays a big part in salmon fishing. In cold water the salmon lies really deep. So Countdown or Deep-Divers do well. Then, as the water temperature rises the salmon seem to come into mid-water and on a hot day are usually found near the surface. So, to sum up on selection: Variation is the key to success of landing your fish.

RIGGING RAPALAS FOR ATLANTIC SALMON

First we attach a split ring or clip directly onto the Rapala, then a leader. Anything from 12″–24″ long and a small swivel between the leader and the line. If any additional weight is required, particularly when using a floater, always place your lead above the swivel on your main line. I, personally, use two types: an anti-kink lead suspended from the swivel or a fold over lead attached to my main line just above the swivel. I use two distinct methods of casting for salmon—up stream and down stream. I usually take up my position at the head of a pool and start to cover the water upstream in an arc, varying my casts in length and depth, but always keeping the Rapala moving slightly faster than the current. One exception is when I fish in white water where I just try to keep in touch with my Rapala by taking up any slack line.

As to the down stream method; I cover the water in exactly the same way, varying the retrieve at different speeds. But I have caught most of my fish while the Rapala is swinging around in an arc across the pool. Then I usually go downstream two or three yards and repeat this pattern of casting. This way one can cover water well.

Local knowledge is important in salmon fishing, or get a good gillie who can point out good salmon lies. To sum up: It is variation of casting and lure selection that will win the day.

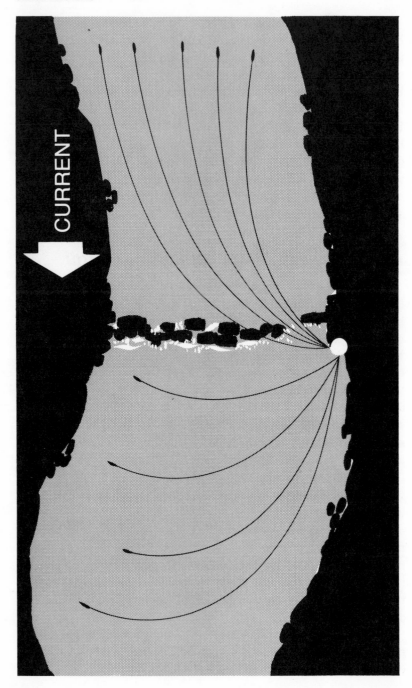

RAPALAS AND SEA TROUT

The sea trout (the anadromous, or sea-run German brown) offers excellent angling in many of the Atlantic salmon rivers of northern Europe, particularly Scandanavia and the British Isles. Much smaller than the Atlantic salmon (three to ten pounds is the usual size), the sea trout is nevertheless one of the very finest gamefish found anywhere.

Pound-for-pound, they fight longer, harder and "smarter" than non-migratory browns, being notorious for their lightning-like jumps, sudden rushes and violent changes of direction. Because of their small size (*vis a vis* the Atlantic salmon), I usually select a size 7 or size 9 Rapala, either original floating or Count-down Model, depending on the depth of the pool that I'm fishing.

Sea trout are best pursued late into the evening because, like the non-migratory browns, they are a cautious, nocturnal feeder. Tidal pools in the lower stretches of rivers seem the favored habitat, or the most likely gathering places where a good population of these strenuous fighters might be found. Angling seems best after a flood tide. They are difficult to entice when the water is low. Discolored water makes for easier angling.

Like many other members of the trout family, these sea-going browns clearly prefer the flourescent red colour. As with the salmon, I usually cast my Rapala upstream and then retrieve it just a shade faster than the current, through the big tidal pools and other likely holding areas. Some of these pools are quite deep during and right after the flood, permitting the using of the Count-down model. In shallower stretches, use the original floater.

Which ever Rapala you select, be ready! The strike will be unmistakeable and the following battle will be long, fierce and unpredictable. Don't say that I didn't warn you!

SPIDER ANDRESEN

Spider Andresen was born and brought up on the ocean. He cut his angling teeth on striped bass at the age of 4 and has been fishing hard ever since. He received his Captains license from the Coast Guard at the age of 18 and has skippered commercial and charter fishing boats from Martha's Vineyard to the Florida Keys and the Bahamas. He has fished the Atlantic and Pacific and has caught many oceanic and litoral gamefish from both sides. While more at ease with striped bass on his home fishing grounds of the Vineyard, he is happiest poling the flats of Key West with a fly rod in search of big tarpon. Spider is the advertising director of Salt Water Sportsman Magazine.

OFFSHORE FISHING IN THE NORTHEAST

Fishermen by nature will often guard a new found secret more closely than a two-century old family heirloom. So it was when the new Rapala CD-18 Deep Diver first was imported to the northeast. There was an American copy of the lure in use at the time, and indeed it was effective. But some had discovered the CD-18 and were returning ashore with larger than average catches. They were not, however, about to divulge the reason why. When two boats fished alongside one another, one using the American lure and one using the Rapala, the Rapala boat would outfish the other. The man with the American lure would watch closely as the Rapala boat would land fish. The two lures looked very similar, and he could only assume the two boats were using the same lure. Furthermore, when questioned, the Rapala user would lie, saying he was using the American copy. It was easy to get away with for they did look alike—except for that incredible swimming lip! I'm not an engineer, so it may be a lot more than the lip of the CD-18, but that's the most visible difference. It has to be one of the major factors that create the phenomenal vibration that draws gamesters to Rapalas like cudas to a shrimp tank.

In the Northeast where striped bass and blue fish are the most commonly sought after gamefish, the Rapala has proved itself time and again. Deep water fishing (3-10 fathoms) is commonplace from New Jersey to Maine. Wire line is employed to get the trolled lure deep to the fish. The combination of the Rapala CD-18's deep swimming lip, it's sinking ability and wire line enables you to go just about as deep as you need to.

As in all fishing, local knowledge and "Yankee ingenuity" can make a good thing better. The success of Grandma Flanders

and the CD-18 on Martha's Vineyard has been nationally publiciz-
ed. One might suspect that there had been some customizing and,
indeed, there has been. Just how effective it has been is illustrated
in the photo which was part of a Rapala ad, shown at the beginning of this article. The list of prizes the Flanders family has won is
impressive—also incomplete. This past season Herbert Hancock
again won the bluefish division of the Martha's Vineyard Derby
with a 17 pound fish, while taking second place in the striped bass
division with a whopping 45 pounder. Both fish were taken on
CD-18's. How does he do it?

First of all, he puts in the time. Herbert is usually the first one
clear of the dock before sunrise and often returns in the dark.
He is obviously a good fisherman and spends his time in the right
area. "Customizing" the lure itself has become a fairly regular
practice. Where voracious 15-20 pound bluefish with atomic
powered jaws and lightening sharp teeth maraud, it has been
discovered that larger hooks catch more fish with little or no loss
of swimming action. The standard 3/0 hooks that come on the
Rapala are replaced by 4/0's. The tail hook is often dressed with

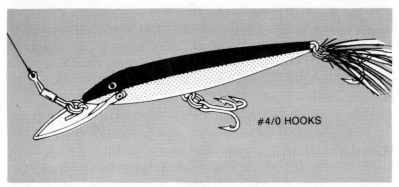

#4/0 HOOKS

deer hair in the form of a bucktail. Sometimes a U-clip is attached
to the bow snapring and bent at a 45 degree angle as pictured.
Some feel this sends the deep-diver even deeper. It should perhaps
be noted here that the "CD" part of the designated CD-18 stands
for "count down." That is, the angler casts the sinking plug out
and allows the plug to sink while counting down before starting
the retrieve. The plug will then maintain the depth it is at when
the retrieve commences. The Rapala's ability to hold an even

deep running depth is one of it's most lauded characteristics. While New England has its share of great surface fishing when one can use the floating Rapala, the men are separated from the boys when the fish aren't feeding on top. This is when the pros get out the wire line and clip on the CD-18's

In New England wire line is as common as down riggers are on the Great Lakes. Down Riggers may well replace wire line in the salt chuck, but the conversion will be slower than it was in fresh water. At any rate, Yankee striped and bluefishermen use 40 to 60 pound test single strand wire line. The favorite is manufactured out of monel and is quite pliable. One usually has a 10 foot mono leader followed by one to three hundred feet of wire line, and then 60 pound test monofiliment backing. At an average trolling speed of three to four knots, 100 feet of trolled 50 pound test wire will take a Rapala CD-18 down about 18 feet. Lengthen the troll to 200 feet and the Rapala will be cruising about 30 feet beneath the surface. With the full 300 feet of wire extended the lure will dive about 43 feet. These depths will vary according to trolling speed, but they are pretty accurate estimates.

Race Point, which is the very tip of Massachusetts' Cape Cod next to Provincetown, has become a well known hot spot for big chopper blues. Fishing on the ocean side a pilgrim could head for Race Point and start trolling right at the tip. The best depth is in about 30 feet of water, and one could expect to find blues anywhere from the tip to three miles up the beach. If the fish are on or near the surface their ungentlemanly feeding habits will make them readily visible. Herring gulls and terns will be diving on the driven bait, and the surface will be covered with flying white water and frenzied feeding fish. Fish will actually clear the surface jumping after fleeing bait. The floating Rapala is obviously the answer in a situation like this. Unfortunately, it is not always that simple.

If there aren't any fish showing, I would start by trolling a CD-18 about 75 feet behind the boat. If nothing happens, drop the lure back to about 100 feet, then to 150 feet, and finally to almost 200 feet, which will have your lure skimming along very close to the bottom. Watch your depthfinder and stay in about 30 feet of water. Somewhere on your way down you'll discover the depth the blues are hanging at and the action will start. If you get the full 200 feet out and are trolling close to the bottom, don't be surprised to haul back a striper, cod, goosefish, fluke, or even a small tuna now and then. The Rapala mimics a myriad of baitfish that frequent the Race Point area and will be attacked by numerous species. When you do fish the right depth and start bringing the choppers to boat, you should be well equipped for handling them and boat blues with caution and respect. A gaff with a three inch hook and at least a three foot handle is necessary. Nets are a waste of time and will be quickly destroyed by the blues. A billy club for subduing the critter is a must and a long handled pair of pliers is a great aid for removing hooks from sharp teeth. They didn't get the knickname "choppers" for their gentle spirit or lack of dentures. This author's right thumb is half an inch|shorter than his left—the price paid when unhooking a bluefish without knocking him out.

Blues retain an amazing amount of fight which they display after being boated. If possible, it is desirable to gaff the fish near the head. This gives you more control while the fish is thrashing about the deck and will also keep good eating filets from having gaff holes in them. A few good whacks with the club to the fishes head will quiet him and is actually a humane way of dispatching the critter. Then one can slide a hand in the gills and take a firm grip before removing the hooks with the pliers. Another favorite grip is from the top of the head with the thumb in one gill plate and the fingers in the other. The arms should be extended and the fish held away from the face and body. Should the fish thrash you want to be clear of flying hooks.

While Race Point is one of the new hot spots, Noman's Land Island just south of Martha's Vineyard has been a standard bluefish and bass ground for decades. Here the search procedure for what depth the fish are at is about the same but executed in the opposite manner. The fish are again on the ocean side of the Island. One starts trolling in 60 feet of water using 300 feet of wire and works his way to shore, shortening up his trolled line as the water becomes shallower. Often the fish will be found in the deep water, and that is obviously why one begins his trolling there. There are other times when casting a floating Rapala into the surf in the same area brings a blue to boat on a one fish to one cast ratio. Under these circumstances I have found the blue floater to be the most effective lure.

While the role that color plays in catching fish varies from day to day, there is a general rule of thumb used by anglers in the northeast. That is a dark plug for grey days, and a light (or blue) plug for bright days. When menhaden are running, a favorite northeast baitfish with flecks of gold on them, the CD-18 with the gold belly works best. In general, good fishermen keep a good supply of all colors of Rapalas on board. Often they will start the day with a black-backed silver Rapala on one rod and blue on the other. One of them will usually take more fish, and the skipper will then fish both lures of that color.

As in all salt water fishing, the peak catching period is likely during the peak tide run. Slack tide is a time of rest. Gulls sit around on the surface waiting for the tide to turn. Gorged fish rest in the depths and fishermen eat sandwiches, drink beer and doze. This is the hour of the Rapala. Time and time again when fishing is slow and nothing is producing fish, the CD-18 will turn the trick. I know some excellent northeastern fishermen that will only use their own homemade bucktail jigs when the tide is running, but switch to the Rapala as soon as the tide slacks off.

Regardless of where one is fishing or whether or not he is using larger hooks, bent U-clip or bucktails, the fact remains that the Rapala is basically a well designed, well built lure that has an action fish like. The lure catches fish. Different Rapala's will work better in different areas, but no tackle box is complete without a good selection of these time proven artificial lures, the Rapalas.

MARK SOSIN

*Recognized as an angling authority in both fresh water and salt,
Mark Sosin has fished extensively on four continents and is well
known for his thoroughly researched, factual presentations. He is
equally at home on a cascading trout stream or aboard blue water
big game craft and has gained fame as a light tackle specialist
with emphasis on artificial lure fishing. He can handle any type
of tackle with equal skill.*

*As a fulltime writer and consultant specializing in fishing tackle
and techniques, his articles have appeared in all of the major
outdoor magazines and he has written an impressive number of
books and booklets. In addition to his writings, he has appeared on
radio, television, and in outdoor motion pictures. Sosin is a Vice
President of the Outdoor Writers Association of America, a
member of the American Society of Journalists and Authors, and
has been elected to The Fishing Hall of Fame.*

THE MIDDLE AND
SOUTH ATLANTIC COAST

You might say that I backed into my love affair with Rapalas. It happened on the Pacific side of Central America several years ago on one of those rare days when every species of gamefish seemed to be suffering from an acute case of lockjaw and, in spite of the testimonials in the travel brochures, the action was as cold and unappealing as yesterday's coffee.

To add to the frustration, the water looked perfect: green swells brushing against a myriad of small islands and jagged rocks with white water swirling at the knees of these obstacles. Huge rocks lurked beneath the surface, sometimes baring their baldness as a wave receded in a sizzle of foam that sounded like a steak broiling on an open grill. There were fish in these very spots yesterday and they would probably be there tomorrow, but the challenge was today.

There's not much one can do under those circumstances but clean out the tackle box and hope. Near the bottom, two unused Rapalas caught my eye and I tied one on. Frankly, I can't remember whether it was the gold or silver colored model, but it didn't matter because on about the fourth cast, it disappeared when a hole suddenly opened in the water's surface. A tail the size of a big electric typewriter flipflopped in the air for an instant and then crash dived for the safety of the depths. The excitement didn't last long. In seconds, the line went limp and my Rapala was gone forever.

The second lure lasted longer and it accounted for a few fish before it, too, suffered a similar fate and was buried at sea. The action was not torrid, but the important fact is that the Rapalas turned up a few fish including some heavyweights while the other lures in the box went fishless. That's when I decided to always carry a few wherever I fished and, over the years, I have learned to lean on them more and more in both fresh water and salt.

Along the Middle Atlantic Coast, striped bass and bluefish rank as the two most popular species for the artificial lure enthusiasts and Rapalas are a natural for this type of sport. Depending on your preference, you can either cast or troll. It's been my experience that because Rapalas are tested at the factory, almost all of them run true and you don't have to worry about tuning them once you are on the water.

Although bluefish will tend to chop at any offering regardless of size, there are times when they will specialize in a certain size bait for feeding efficiency. Striped bass, of course, follow this pattern even more. For that reason, you should have an assortment of Rapalas in various sizes and you should include both floating and sinking models.

Casters often overlook the Countdown models for stripers and blues, yet these lures offer distinct advantages in making presentations under a variety of conditions. Even when bass or blues are breaking on the surface, I prefer to get a bait a few feet under. For one thing, it's easier for a fish to inhale it and, for another, you get more strikes. Sometimes, you only need to let it sink a foot or two, but when the fish start to go down, you can wait several seconds and get the lure down to fisheye level. The Countdown model gives you flexibility and that can be important.

In Chesapeake Bay and other estuaries along the coast where school size rock (stripers) will shoulder under overhanging sod banks and precision casting is important, the Countdown can make a difference. You can toss it against the bank, let it sink an instant or two, and then start the retrieve. By letting it sink, you allow the lure to come into the fish's window of vision and it is easier for your quarry to grab it. Most anglers will use a surface plug and that means it has to be pulled away from the bank before the fish can hit it.

The fish-like shape of the Rapala imitates a variety of baitfish that are common in this part of the country. Size, however, is the key. You should attempt to match the length of the lure to the length of the natural bait in the area. If that doesn't work, then try a longer lure. Extensive research with bluefish, for example, has shown that when the fish appear to be completely satiated on smaller bait, they will turn on again when they are offered larger prey.

When you locate a school of blues or stripers on the surface with gulls and terns shrieking and diving above them, it's one of the most exciting experiences in angling. The best approach is to keep your boat off to one side of the school so that you don't put the fish down and cast right into the main body. If you are trolling, ease the boat down one edge and then swing out so that the boat clears the fish but the lines sweep into the center of activity. You'll discover that there are plenty of fish on the fringes and they will strike very quickly.

Since a gamefish must isolate its prey in order to attack, a lure that "escapes" from a school of baitfish and seems to wander off on its own is almost certain to become a victim. Gamesters wait for the stragglers or bait that becomes disoriented. Also, a lure that looks slightly different than the natural bait is easier for a fish to see and zero in on.

The Magnum Rapalas should be your first choice for big stripers and the huge bluefish that have been prowling the coastline for the past several years. I switch between floating and sinking models depending on what I am trying to achieve and where the fish might be. Over rocky terrain for old linesides, for example, I would favor the floater because it will come back to the surface if I stop the retrieve or put the boat in neutral. In deeper tide rips or when bluefish are sulking, the sinking models are a better choice.

Because these lures are made out of wood and wired through, the infamous dentures of bluefish or even barracuda can't puncture them and cause the baits to leak. That's one of the drawbacks of hollow plastic lures on toothy fish. Once the bait is punctured, it fills with water and loses its action.

Weakfish have been making a significant comeback of late from Delaware Bay to Peconic Bay and a number of trophy fish have been taken. Prime action begins in the late spring and fish are taken through the summer months. In the fall, the weakies gather off the beachfronts and begin a southerly migration that also offers peak action.

The Countdown Rapalas are a perfect choice and, when the fish are fairly deep, you may want to go to a deep diving Rapala. Experiment with a variety of sizes. The size 7 and 9 will produce best on most fish, but you may want an even longer offering for some of the tiderunners that have been taken. These same baits will also work for sea trout farther south and can be used in the surf during the fall when the trout sweep along the beachfronts. That's the time for small plugs, light spinning rods or bait casting outfits, and a pair of waders.

There are a number of different ways to rig and fish Rapalas, but it all boils down to confidence and feel. You have to believe in the lure and its ability to catch fish. No artificial can perform miracles. If you give it a fair chance, however, and learn to use it effectively, you'll develop confidence and you'll know when the lure is working correctly.

Many anglers use a snap swivel or just a snap to attach a Rapala. This enables the lure to swing from side to side and have a degree of flexibility, limited, of course, by the size of the snap. If I use terminal tackle such as swivels and snaps, I want them to be as small and inconspicuous as possible. For species such as small striped bass and weakfish, I would probably use a snap and tie it directly to my light casting line without any leader. When larger bass are present, I tend to favor a light shock leader of perhaps 20 to 30 pound test.

Somewhere in this game of fishing you must reach a compromise. It has always been my belief that the lighter the line and leader you use, the more strikes you will get. With toothy creatures such as bluefish, kingfish, mackerel, and barracuda, you have to make a decision. If you use a wire leader on blues, you will probably get fewer strikes. This may not be noticeable on the good days, but it will certainly get your attention the rest of the time. You run the risk, of course, of losing lures if you don't use wire. I try to play it down the middle, choosing heavy monofilament as protection against those dentures.

With species such as wahoo, kingfish, and barracuda, you may lose the plug more times than not if you don't use wire. Again I try to compromise. I'll use about a foot of wire and then make the rest of the leader monofilament. That short trace of wire will give me protection against the dentures, but the mono will help to produce more strikes. If fishing is particularly slow, I may eliminate the wire altogether and gamble the plug against some action. If I'm lucky and the fish strikes short, it's score one on my team, but if that critter is salivating as he closes the distance on my bait, he'll probably engulf the whole thing and he owns the plug.

Proper rigging is extremely important. Except in extreme situations, I always use a Bimini Twist in the end of my casting or trolling line. Then, I either use a Double Surgeon's Knot or an Albright to attach any shock leader including plastic coated wire. The Double Surgeon's Knot is best when the heavier line is 3 to 4 times heavier than the lighter line. With a greater difference or for single strand wire, the Albright is the answer. You'll also discover that the Spider Hitch may be quicker to tie than the Bimini, but it could fail under impact or the shock of a sudden pull.

Learning to feel a lure on the retrieve or know when the trolling speed is correct becomes a matter of experience coupled with plenty of trial and error. No one can really tell you the answers, but there are a few guidelines that you may find helpful. If you remember that there are no surefire methods that work every day on all species of fish, you're already ahead of the game. The trick is to experiment and think about what you are doing so that when you do get a strike, you can repeat the exact performance.

Usually, I'll start with a straight retrieve at a medium rate of speed. In a current, I'll crank a bit slower and, when the waters are placid, I may speed up just a bit. During a single cast, I may start slowly, build up speed, pause an instant, and continue cranking. One thing that I tend to do is vibrate the hand holding the rod just a little and at irregular intervals. This causes the lure to turn on its side for an instant and creates a "flash" that can make the difference.

The best way to learn to fish a Rapala or any other lure is to cast it in a swimming pool or make short casts in clear water where you can watch the action. Then, try a number of different retrieves. Watch what happens when you pause or when you crank fast and then slow down or when you vibrate the wrist. Once you've seen the effect, you can picture what is taking place below the surface on those long blind casts.

Continue to vary the retrieve while you are fishing until you discover what the fish prefer at that particular time. When the fish stop striking, start experimenting with retrieves again and vary speed and action until you begin to score once more. If you insist on casting and retrieving without thought or game plan, you're not getting the full measure of performance from your artificials.

Trolling offers the same challenges and experienced anglers always take the time to learn how a bait will perform at various speeds. Hold the lure close to the boat and watch it swim. Vary the engine settings until you find the slowest speed at which it will have fish appeal and the fastest. Try the lure moving with the current, across the current, and against the flow of the water. See what happens if you sweep the rod forward and then let the plug fall back as the boat continues to move. Once you have a mental picture of what is taking place behind the boat, you know the effect of different throttle settings and rod actions. If you intend to catch fish with any lure, you better learn precisely how it works and what it can do.

Rapalas have equal validity on the offshore grounds as well as near the beach. You can troll them behind a sportfisherman and pick up everything from wahoo to dolphin and tuna to bonito. If you are using natural baits on your primary lines, try a Rapala in close between 30 and 50 feet behind the boat. Rig it on a 30 pound outfit or lighter and you should find yourself busy with a grabbag of species.

Offshore fishing can be opportunity sport and it always makes sense to have casting tackle rigged and ready. While someone is fighting a fish, others may appear near the boat and there's always a chance to pick off some of the action if you have a rod handy. Dolphin are a prime example. You can either hold the hooked fish in the water and attract others or, under some circumstances, you can keep a school off the stern by tossing small pieces of chum. Even though dolphin are truly crowd pleasers, they can be selective when they are near a boat. One of the best techniques is to make long casts beyond the fish that you see and then bring the lure back toward you at a fairly fast rate. Dolphin have amazing eyesight and they can run down an offering faster than you can read this.

The same approach sometimes works on other species of fish. If you cast in the area after a blind strike from wahoo, kingfish, bonito, tuna, or others, you can often pick up a fish on light gear that you didn't even know was in the area. It's a matter of being prepared and getting the lure into the water quickly.

Rapalas are also deadly over a reef. Trollers have the option of dragging them relatively close to the surface or using weights or downriggers to get them down over the coral outcroppings. The variety of fish that will strike these plugs is staggering and you'll catch everything from grouper to barracuda. Magnum sizes should be first choice because reef dwellers get rather large and can engulf those plugs with ease.

If you're trolling, there are a few techniques worth remembering. The dropoff side of a reef can be particularly productive and you can work back and forth along the edge. Check the direction of the current and work against it first and then with it. You should throttle down a bit against the current and just let the lure work back and forth. As you approach a reef, there are days when you will catch more fish by trolling from the deep into and over the reef. At other times, you'll do better by dragging the lures from the shallower reef over the deep. The trick is to stay alert and recognize what has happened and what you are doing when you get a strike. Then, repeat the pattern.

Casting a reef can be a great deal of fun. Move up wind or up current and let the boat drift along. Casts should be long and vary the retrieve until you find the combination. Frequently, you'll find bait balled up over a reef and it's easy to make long presentations, fanning each cast in the area to cover the water thoroughly. Marine predators can hit that lure from a long distance. Mackerel and kingfish will sometimes greyhound through the air and land right on the plug or lunge skyward from the depths and pick it off on the way up. It's been my experience that faster retrieves do a better job on these fast swimmers. Tuna and bonito also prefer a rapidly moved bait.

Weedlines are another source of action and you can either troll along them or work down the line and cast toward the weeds.

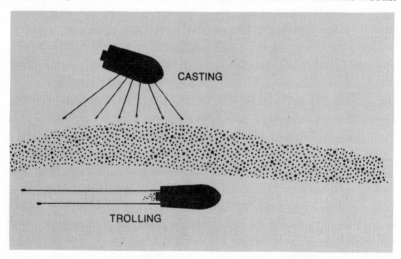

With a pair of polarized sunglasses, you can often spot cruising fish near the weeds and make your presentations to a specific target. Dolphin, of course, will seek these weedlines and you'll find them under any type of flotsam. Flip a Rapala toward them and you should be in business.

When you work an artificial lure near any fish you can see, it is well to remember that predators are not in the habit of being attacked by their prey. For some reason, anglers want to pull a bait toward a gamefish, hoping that their quarry will see the offering. Instead, they sometimes frighten the very fish they want to catch because they create an unnatural situation.

One variation that sometimes produces fish is to cast beyond the target and start the lure toward you rather slowly. Then, as if the prey had sighted the predator, speed up the retrieve and try to take the lure away. This will often tease the gamefish into striking.

Speaking of teasing, you can sometimes work with a hookless live bait over a reef or wreck to tease up cobia, amberjack, barracuda, and other species. By pulling the natural bait away from the heavyweights and sometimes letting an amberjack or cobia wrap its lips around the goodie, you can turn those fish on. Then, it's merely a matter of tossing a Rapala out there and having your quarry climb all over it.

No artificial lure is a panacea for every angling ill and there isn't a bait in the world that is foolproof or will never fail to catch fish. Some, however, have a track record of producing rather consistently in all of the waters of the world. Rapalas fall into this category. The day that I cleaned my tackle box in Central America, I convinced myself that it pays to carry an assortment of Rapalas. They work on a variety of gamefish in salt water and can be cast or trolled with equal effectiveness. There may be a day when you'll be glad you had a few in your box, no matter where you do most of your fishing.

KEN LAUER

Like other great guides, Ken Lauer is one of the important innovators. In this story he tells how he and his associates brought the Rapala to the Outer Banks and southeastern costal waters; how they captured record amounts of saltwater gamefish on this lifelike lure and light tackle.

After retiring from the military in 1968, Ken moved immediately to Cape Hatteras to pursue, full time, his love of fishing. Today, he is co-owner of Outer Banks Safaris, a complete sportfishing service headquartered in Buxton, North Carolina. Its eight beach guides and three deep-water boats provide the angler with complete expertise and access to some of the finest fishing in the world.

In his story, Ken Lauer tells how to fish for three of the most important gamefish which range all the way from Central America, and south, to more northerly stretches of the Atlantic.

FISHING THE SURF AND
SEA OF THE SOUTHEAST U.S.

Those who have called the Outer Banks, composed of Hatteras and Ocracoke islands, one of America's last, great natural frontiers are absolutely right. I would only add that this goes double, in spades!, for the quality of its fishing; both surf and boat.

Like Peru's great Cabo Blanco, the Outer Banks mark the confluence of two major currents extremely rich in fish life. In our case, it's the meeting of the Gulf Stream, pushing up from Florida and swinging close to the mainland before veering out into the Atlantic; and a branch of the Labrador Current, plowing down from Canada.

Striped bass winter off Hatteras. The surrounding waters, depending on the season of the year, abound with king mackerel, bluefish, cobia, weakfish, flounder, croaker and tarpon in addition to the many placid species favored by bottom-fisherman.

But I'm here to talk about the three leading gamefish of our area and points south. They are, in order of presentation, striped bass, bluefish and king mackerel (sometimes called the kingfish.) Each, given the correct knowledge and approach, proves extremely susceptible to the Rapala. No other artificial, in my estimation, takes these fighters like the lifelike lure with a Finnish accent.

The striper is kind of a sometimes thing. Sometimes we have them coming out of our ears, at other times not one is to be found. This is because they are irregular feeders; fasting for long periods of time, then going on feeding rampages during which no baitfish or lure is safe.

I'm pleased to think that I was instrumental in discovering a new fishery when, one silvery, moon-lit January night in 1974, several of us were surf-casting for stripers on Hatteras. At that time, the conventional wisdom was that only live bait, and maybe an occasional metal lure, would catch these fish.

We changed that thinking, in a hurry, by tying the #18 (7 in.) floating Rapala directly to the monofilament surf-casting line and casting into what, that night, was definitely "white" water. We discovered that by retrieving our lures *very slowly*, and letting the current move them, from left to right across the point we were working, the stripers went absolutely crazy.

Three of us caught 1,000 pounds of striped bass that first night on large floating silver Rapalas, casting up-current from our point, then reeling in very slowly, letting the motion of the rod tip and the force of the current create a lure action like nothing else in fishing. Today, this is a standard approach. And nothing is more exciting: stripers up to 40 lbs. peeling 100 yards of line off your reel as they make that first run down the beach, then battling in every foot of the way!

A word on fighting these fish: be very patient, take your time. Let the current help you. Succeeding runs become shorter and shorter. Really big bass sometimes position themselves broadside to the retrieve. Walk your fish around until a good-sized breaker carries the striper shoreward. Then make your move when he's high and dry! Don't let another comber rescue your fish. Also, lots of surf-casters lose stripers because of too-tight reel drag. A 20 pound bass can part a line twice that strong. So keep a reasonable drag and enjoy fighting your fish.

I don't want to leave the impression that surf-fishing for stripers is confined to nocturnal hours. During the day, it can be even more fun. When I detect signs of feeding bass (frantic bait-fish, congregating birds), I present the smaller, #13 floating Rapala tied, without terminal tackle, to an 8 or 12 pound mono line. You can actually see when some of the daytime stripers hit, often in only 3 or 4 feet of water. The battle is really joined when it's a 30 or 40 pound bass, certainly not unheard of with this technique. What I like about the #13 Rapala is the ability of its razor-sharp hooks to get into a striper's mouth very easily. There is no need to set the hook unduly hard. Remember to keep the drag set just ahead of the setting-point of your hooks. Then it's a matter of hanging in there: having complete faith in your tackle and knowing it's going to do the job you've set out to do.

Of course, stripers will also strike subsurface and deep-running lures. Surf-casting from a small boat is done in our area, but Outer Banks sea conditions can mean trouble to the novice. Therefore, we strongly suggested that the caster operate from a boat skippered by an experienced local guide. When casting from a boat, propel the lure in toward the beach and retrieve through the white water. When using this on-shore approach, try floating Magnum Rapalas in the larger sizes, #13 and #18, because you will now have more water to work with.

BLUEFISH

Although smaller than striped bass, blues are stronger, faster and meaner. And beware! In addition to possessing a razor-sharp set of teeth, they also see as well out of the water as in it, so their bite is invariably well-directed and very painful. Handle with care!

This same truculent disposition makes the blue a heart-stopping gamefish when taken on surf or light boat tackle. Because of its dynamite fighting ability and sharp teeth, I find it imperative to use a short, 4 to 6 inch metal leader between my

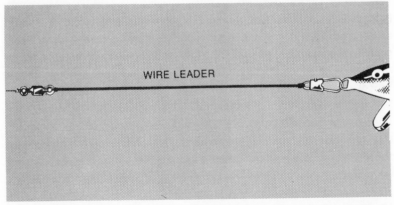

WIRE LEADER

line and Rapala: with the smallest feasible snaps and swivels so as not to unduly restrict the wiggling action of the lure. I've found that a half-foot leader neither kinks nor interferes unduly with the cast. And because we sometimes troll for "choppers" at up to 12 knots, swivels are necessary in case a heavy sea causes the lure to broach.

But surf-casting is the preferred method; fall and winter the best seasons for encountering the 10 to 20 pound blues then patrolling our shores. Early morning and late evening are the best times to angle for these fish, as they are for most saltwater species.

Tide, wind, weather and water conditions must also be taken into account. In heavy or murky water, the flourescent red Rapala works best. When the water is more calm and clear, the silver and blue colors seem to take more fish. Size of the lure varies with the depth of the water fished.

The areas I like best are the shallow "sloughs" that lie between the off-shore bar and the beach. These depressions are 25 to 35 yards in width and hold water anywhere from 4 to 6 feet in depth. The bluefish come into these sloughs to feed on baitfish, driving all before them as they rip, slash, maim and kill everything in their path. I have actually stood in such sloughs with big blues on every side of me; many feeding to the rear, practically up on the beach. When the choppers are in this mood, nothing in the water is safe. But the Rapala really proves its versatility when the fish are dispersed and must be teased into taking a lure.

We have devised a technique for this kind of fishing. It consists of taking a floating Rapala, either original or Magnum (you might have to experiment a bit here) casting it into a slough or rip and then using a special retrieve. Here is how I do it: pick up your line and lure briskly and send it to the bottom with a fast retrieve. Then stop suddenly, allowing the plug to float about half-way up to the surface. Then repeat the entire process, simulating the "jerking" motion of a wounded baitfish that almost makes it to the bottom and then weakens to float back toward the top. This has an especially galvanizing affect on bluefish and goads them into striking when other methods fail. Blues lying in a rip will often ignore a fast-moving lure; but a stuttering, stop-and-go Rapala seems to work magic.

We have also found that the Rapala adds a new dimension to trolling for blues. Again, water conditions play a major part in selection of the lure and trolling speed. While some skippers prefer to troll at 5 to 8 knots for bluefish, we have found that higher speeds often yield bigger pay-offs with the Rapala. This is made possible, in large part, by the lure's superior stability and anti-broaching characteristics which permit a faster pace on the outer stretches.

In calm water, we have determined that 12 knots is a good trolling speed for both blues and king mackerel. At this pace, we can keep a large floating Rapala just under the surface on 60 to 70 feet of line. If the fish prove to be deeper, then we switch to a planer or down-rigger, at which juncture I dip into the tackle box and select the metal-lipped sinking Magnum. I am anxious to try the new silver mackerel finish. It would appear to be an excellent color for clear water conditions.

If there's a moderate chop on the water, I cut back to 8 or 9 knots, so the planer or down-rigger can ride comfortably and any motion induced by these devices is not conducted to the lure, which might cause it to broach. These higher speeds seem not only to catch more blues, but also tend to keep the sharks off our lines. Sharks are considered a nuisance fish here and are not prized by most of our anglers.

Newcomers to bluefishing sometimes make the mistake of chasing surfaced schools of fish or trolling through the center of such a group. It's almost certain that the school will sound immediately and stay down because of boat-shyness. It is always better to manuever your boat so your lures pass ahead of the sighted fish and to drift-cast or troll at a steady rate rather than taking off at high-port in pursuit of a surfaced school.

KING MACKEREL

King Mackerel (also called kingfish) seem to prefer the flourescent red Rapala in any water or wave conditions. Unsought by surf-casters, kings nevertheless move in immense offshore schools with individual specimens ranging from 8 to 24 pounds: The larger kingfish, running from 30 to 40 pounds, are often more scattered than the "schoolers" and definitely prefer the Rapala over all other trolled artificials. We usually find the big kings over 40 to 50 feet of water, although they will occasionally move in to depths in the 20's.

When fishing for kings, the usual procedure it to use down-riggers or planers with the sinking Magnum or Deep-Diver Rapala, with a short, swiveled metal leader ahead of the lure.

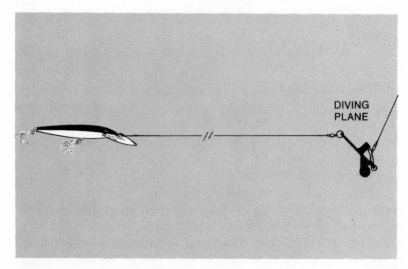

Trolling speeds are as for the blues and good catches are made with the Rapala when all other artificials seem to fail.

Come on down fishing to North Carolina's Hatteras country. You'll find some of the finest angling and friendliest people in the world. And be sure to look me up. I'll be glad to tell you where they're hitting and the proper equipment to use.

JED WELSH

Question: To whom would one turn as the best source of "one stop" fishing information about the West Coast—from San Francisco Bay to the Baja Peninsula by way of inland trout streams and lunker largemouth impoundments?

Answer: Indubitably, Jed Welsh! When a boy, Jed worked in his father's tackle factory and guided trout parties in the High Sierras. As a young resident of Catalina Island, he would inveigle his way on board the off-shore fishing boats. Jed, now a resident of Long Beach, owned his own terminal tackle factory for 36 years, developing such effective baits as the "Breakwater Spec'l" and "Psychedelic Marlin Lure."

He tries to fish at least 100 days a year and until recently held the International Game Fish Association's world record for rooster-fish, when it was broken by a fishing companion. A trusted friend and compadre of many Mexican commercial hand-line fishermen, Jed has recorded a number of outstanding sportfishing exploits: taking three marlin in one morning on 20-pound test line; capturing 100 pound sailfish on a light, basscasting outfit rigged with 12-pound line. As if to prove his all-water capability, Jed recently won first place in a Lake Mojave largemouth tournament. He touches all of those bases, and many more, in the following roundup story on West Coast fishing.

FISHING IN BAJA AND CALIFORNIA WATERS

The realization that the Rapala is a deadly lure in salt water has changed the trolling picture in Southern California and Baja Mexico completely in the last 3 years. We had always used up our old bass plugs in Baja and caught fish. Accidentally or not, someone started using a Rapala and it was immediately evident that it was much superior to any other lure. It's hard to believe how many fish will "climb onto" a Rapala first when it is trolled side by side with other lures, but I have tried and proven it so many times against so many others that there's just no doubt about it any more.

All game fish on both sides of the Baja Peninsula will take a Rapala. Of course it is difficult to hook a marlin or sailfish since they strike the lure with their hard bill to kill it and don't eat it; however, in about one strike out of ten, the hooks do manage to snag someplace in the head area.

MEXICO

As a general rule, a medium to slow troll gets the best results in rocky areas. The types of fish that live here are more or less in hiding, waiting for prey to swim by their area. Average from 3 to 5 knots.

RAPALA TROLLING SPEEDS - WEST COASTAL WATERS

SPECIES	HABITAT	SPEED
Reef fish	Rocky areas	3 to 5 knots
Roosterfish, corbina, needle-fish, sierra, etc.	Sandy bottoms	5 to 7 knots
Albacore, yellowtail, dolphin, tuna, skipjack wahoo, etc.	Deep water	6 to 8½ knots

---

In open sandy beaches where the roosterfish, corbina, needle-fish, sierra, etc., feed, more speed will pay off. We have found that speeds of 5 to 7 knots bring best results. Don't use sinkers ahead of your Rapalas when over rocks. It causes loss of lures and is not necessary to bring the fish up out of their lairs. Over sandy areas, first troll without weights, and this is usually all that's needed. If results are slow, add heavy enough sinkers to almost reach bottom and even occasionally bump the bottom. If this fails, move to another beach where there may be more baitfish and more action.

In deep, open blue water troll just as fast as the Rapala can travel without spinning or jumping. From 6 to 8½ knots is very productive. Dolphin fish (Dorado) tuna, skip-jack, albacore, wahoo, etc., are all very excitable fish and are used to chasing fast moving bait.

Members of the jack family such as yellowtail, amberjack, African pompano, roosterfish, etc., and wahoo will all take both size 13 and 18 Magnum but the larger fish show a preference for the size 18. Those gamesters belonging to the mackerel family— tuna, sierra, albacore, skipjack, etc., are used to feeding on smaller baitfish. The size 13 is always better here. The fabulous dolphin-fish will go after either size and shows no preference, taking all the colors with equal enthusiasm.

One great trick for inducing strikes from dolphin is to cut off about two-thirds of the plastic lip of either #13 or #18. Go fast enough (5 to 7 knots) so the lure goes wild; leaping out, skating on its side, diving in a stream of bubbles, etc. This drives dolphin absolutely nuts and they keep darting and leaping after the elusive Rapala until they get it! It is one of the most exciting ways to fish I have ever experienced. Roosterfish and wahoo will also go berserk for this system. When fishing for wahoo or large sierra, always use wire ahead of the lure as their teeth are razor sharp and if they hit the head of the lure or swallow it completely, you will be out one Rapala. Take plenty with you as they are hard to find in Mexico.

The two colors that work best in Mexican waters are the silver and the fluorescent red. With these two colors in both size 13 and 18 you are covered for just about any piscatorial ambush in the waters of Baja.

TROUT

The smaller sizes work very well for trout in lakes in the Sierras and Southern California. In fact, the largest trout ever caught in California was taken in 1975 on a Rapala. Tie the mono line or leader directly to the lure. Never spoil the action of the appearance of a Rapala by using snaps or snap-swivels. Tie to the lure with a small open loop. This gives freedom of movement and much better action.

In summer when the water warms it is necessary to troll deep; Rapalas behind lead lines, down-riggers, or deep trolling devices will bring best results. During colder months or early mornings and late evenings when the surface water has cooled, troll faster and with no sinkers. During these conditions, keep your lures well behind the boat (75 to 150 ft.). I have usually had more

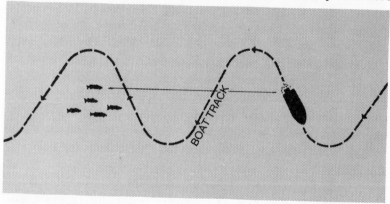

strikes when traveling in slow curves instead of a straight line. This puts the lures through areas that the boat did not actually cover.

An excellent trick when trolling either fresh or salt water in order to control the distance up off the bottom is the following rig: The line is attached to the front of a 3-way swivel and the leader (whatever length you want for the day's conditions) is attached to the other end. Now tie a piece of mono, the length you want to have the lure above the bottom, to the middle eye of the 3-way swivel. Attach a sinker to the bottom of this "hanging" line tight enough so it will hold, but loose enough so it will slide off if caught solidly on snags or bottom. Let out enough line so you can feel the sinker occasionally bump the bottom. With this system always use a floating model Rapala. If the sinker hangs up, the lure will not sink to the bottom and get snagged too.

SAN FRANCISCO BAY - STRIPED BASS

In the area I cover, the most productive place for "stripers" is the San Francisco Bay. Great numbers of these fish in all sizes enter the bay in the early spring and stay until fall. While all systems are used extensively, I would have to say that using live bait or casting and trolling Rapalas are the best. Magnums are recommended, of course, because of their durability and the heavy-duty hooks. The fish in the Bay sometimes reach 35 to 40 lbs., so a lighter-weight fresh-water hook is pretty easy to straighten out.

In the Upper Bay, trolling is most popular. It is generally much deeper there and the outgoing tides create fast-running channels and rips that are perfect spots for large minnow-action lures like Rapalas. Famous areas like Twin Brothers, Twin Sisters, small islands, rocks, and the ends of piers and docks are the hot spots. Troll across current or against the outgoing tides.

The consensus of opinion among experienced anglers here is that the blue color is best. Since the fish feed chiefly on anchovies, herring, and smelt, this is logical. Personally, I have had wonderful fishing with both the silver and the fluorescent red colors at times, too.

The lower part of the Bay offers great sport to both casters and trollers. It is an area of shallower waters interspersed with countless channels of all sizes. During high water the fish are likely to be found most any place, so trolling shallow pays off. Near shore is usually better than out in the middle of the bay unless you know of a "high" spot such as a raised sand bar, mud bank, or sunken structure with drop-off edges that will attract and hold baitfish. Piers, barges, rocky points, are always good areas.

The most sport, I think, is casting to the feeding stripers from shore, while wading or from a small boat. These fish feed voraciously and often. When you spot stripers in a feeding frenzy—whether a few fish or a large school—get to them as soon as you can and drop a floating Rapala (preferably a size 13 Magnum floater) into the area. You will almost always get a boiling, smashing strike.

Rather than retrieving the lure fast, try making it imitate a crippled minnow on, or just under, the surface.

Night fishing here on an out-going tide can be terrific. The fish can often be seen finning and tailing on the surface in their search for food. A floating Rapala (size 13 Magnum) thrown near, or ahead, of such a fish usually results in a charging strike. Here, again, play the lure on the surface to imitate a crippled baitfish. The strikes encouraged under these quiet surface conditions are usually from the larger hungry fish and are not recommended for anglers with weak hearts! A lot of the lakes in Southern California now have striped bass in them. They feed on native minnows, especially thread-fin shad. A silver Rapala is a natural under these conditions. Not a lover of bright sunlight, stripers on the surface usually feed either very early or very late. Unfortunately, night fishing is not allowed in our lakes. A school of stripers will corral a school of shad and work them into the end of a bay or against a steep-walled bank (the face of a dam is a favorite spot).

Watch for surface-feeding action and get there quickly. Casting to these fish is much better than trying to troll through them. These fish are eager to strike and the silver Rapala fools them completely. Recently on San Luis Reservoir, three of us in two morning sessions took 135 bass!

LARGEMOUTH BASS

There has been so much written about black-bass fishing with Rapalas that I don't feel I can actually add anything for our area. Rapalas work very well as they do everywhere for bass. Other than the usual systems, I'll mention my two pet tricks. Near heavy surface cover, let your Rapala (silver if the predominant food-fish are shad; gold if they are chubs, perch, carp, etc.), lie still after casting until all the ripples have subsided. Now shake the rod-tip to make it quiver; pause, then jerk lure forward with two or three short movements; pause, and pull under for 3 or 4 swimming wiggles and let float to surface. If you don't get struck within 3 repetitions of the above, cast to another fishy looking spot. During the spawning periods when the fish are on the "beds", use Deep-Diver Rapalas. Reel fast enough through a spawning bed area so you can feel the lip of the plug actually "chugging" along on the bottom. This may seem like a kind of a dirty trick, but it will sure get you a lot of big bass!

SALTWATER TROLLING

The Rapala lure has completely changed the saltwater trolling picture in Southern California in the last few years. Fifty years ago many fish were caught by trolling; then came the advent of the live-bait tank. Trolling (except with lead-head feather jigs for albacore) was forgotten. Everyone chummed and fished with live bait. Even the famous albacore was only trolled for long enough to locate a school.

A few of us had never given up trolling around the kelp beds and points for kelp bass with plugs of various kinds. We always took plenty to eat. When we started using Rapalas, we not only caught a lot more bass but occasionally hooked a barracuda, bonito, or yellowtail, even though we were fishing in or near kelp bass areas.

One of my favorite fishing companions, Phil Greyshock

(President of the Quick Reel Corp.) finally said, "Hey, Jed, these lures work so well in Mexico and on bass, let's go down to San Diego and really try 'em hard for yellowtail." The famous fighting "yellows" were averaging between 12 and 25 lbs. Lots were being taken on live squid from the big live-bait boats. No other baits were working, not even live anchovies, smelt, or mackerel. We trolled No. 13 and 18 Magnum Rapalas to no avail; then tried spoons, jigs, feathers, bone-jigs, and artificial squids—no go here either. We put our old-faithful Rapalas back out and we could see an occasional yellow or two following but not taking. Then some good bird and surface action showed up a hundred yards away. Without bringing in the lures, we speeded up to about 8½ knots to run to the hot spot. Before we got there we had a double strike. Bingo! We finally had the answer—a very fast troll with Rapalas was it! Since we so cleverly had accidentally stumbled upon the secret we have become famous. Really, we average way more fish per rod every time out than any of the boats using live squid, anchovies, etc. This system is catching on fast now and more and more private boats are fast trolling Rapalas—getting more good fish with less trouble than they ever used to dream possible. All colors work but blue seems to be the least productive. Phil and I had a No. 13 Gold Magnum Sinker that had taken over 100 yellowtail until a small-medium mako shark decided he liked it too.

Albacore are the most sought after gamefish in Southern California waters. They usually migrate into our reach near the first of July and stay until late October. They are caught by trolling feather jigs and by live anchovies. The feather jigs come in all color combinations, sizes, weights, and different head materials; pearl, inlaid abalone, shell, silver, gold, plastic, cedar, and colors of all kinds are experimented with continuously to keep up with the changing tastes of these exotic fish.

I have fished for them ever since I lived at Catalina Island as a small boy and went out at every possible chance as an alleged "helper" on my father's friends' boats. I have seen hundreds of tons of albacore caught but I had never seen one caught on any kind of a "plug" type lure until last year, 1975. Phil and I were in a pretty good albacore spot and had caught a couple early on live bait, but then the "bite" shut off. The fish were still there, we could

tell by the bird action and the leaping baitfish. We trolled through and over them for two hours with all kinds of feathers and didn't have one hit. "Let's try our yellowtail system". "You have finally flipped—albies don't take bass lures!" "What have we got to lose? They aren't taking anything anyhow!" We put on two No. 13 Magnum Sinkers, one silver and one red fluorescent. In less than five minutes at 8½ knots, we had a solid, double hook-up. Bingo again! We had come across the hottest system for sport trolling for albacore that was ever devised. We took 17 or 18 that morning and no other boat in that small area caught one.

With our newly discovered knowledge we went down to Ensenada, B.C., in our trailered 21' boat. Hard winds forced us in at noon both days, but when we unloaded 59 albacore for three of us, the Mexicans quit laughing at our "stupido" Rapalas and began asking where they could buy some. We have found the best colors are the red fluorescent and the silver, although we have caught fish on both blue and gold, too. Not too heavy a line (12, 15, or 20 pound) and a soft-tip rod give the lures the best action. We troll from 70 to 100 feet back and as fast as we can without causing the lures to spin or jump.

We have been extremely successful using this technique on

albacore. On several trips we even caught blue-fin tuna which are notorious for not taking anything with a hook in it, much less a trolled lure right in the wake. I advise anyone with a private boat fishing in Southern California ocean waters to always have a few Rapalas aboard. They are the best all-around lure I have ever seen. Any fish that chases and eats minnows and baitfish will take them.

Personally, as a life-time ardent angler, I am just thankful for the makers of the Rapala lures. These people have surely spent a long time really trying to make the best lure possible, showing a total dedication to perfection and evidently never a compromise to excellence. So far in the fishing lure business, Rapalas have been many times copied but never equalled.

LARRY SCHOENBORN

When Oregonians think of fishing, they automatically think of Larry Schoenborn, owner and operator of two of the most complete sportfishing centers in the Pacific Northwest. The stores, Larry's Sport Centers, are located in Oregon City and Gresham, Oregon. They provide anglers with all of their needs, including the latest and most authoritative angling advisories from Larry and his courteous staff.

Larry, who began fishing the lakes, streams and Pacific Ocean almost before he could walk, specializes in steelhead trout ... and total service to his customers. He regularly charters group fishing trips to the fabulous waters of nearby British Columbia, trips on which he shares his know-how with those eager to learn from an acknowledged expert. In this story, he shares much of that knowledge.

FISHING IN THE PACIFIC NORTHWEST

In my opinion, the waters of the Pacific Northwest provide one of the greatest assortments of 365-days-a-year angling of any place in the world. Of all of the many species we catch here, the steelhead (migratory rainbow) trout is king. And the Rapala family of fishing lures is the *required* assortment to take along on just about any fishing trip.

I learned about the Rapala from direct experience in 1963. The introduction came when only six lures were shipped to the large, Portland-area sporting goods store of which I was then general manager. All were #7 floating models, gold in color. They were quickly divvied up: one going to each of four employees who more or less specialized in fishing tackle; the other two were sold to customers.

The following Sunday, I took my family on a fishing picnic to a local reservoir, where we were joined by one of the other Rapala owners and his family. They, in fact, arrived first and I didn't catch up to their boat until they'd been fishing for a while. In reply to my inevitable question, "how they hittin'?", the early-bird hefted a string of big rainbows (for that busy suburban lake), all between 18 and 22 inches. In reply to my next question, my fellow-worker rolled his eyes and said, "You won't believe this. But we caught them *all* on that new, uh ... Rapala ... you gave me to try the other day!" Instantly, a legend was born in the Pacific Northwest.

Until that day, the *only* way we could ever catch trout on that impoundment was with a "lake troll" and one of two pieces of terminal tackle: either a wiggling "banana"-type lure or, much more often, a small hook dressed with a piece of earthworm. With either of those lures, a 12 or 14 inch rainbow was the norm.

Here, he had a whole stringer-full of trout, the *smallest* of them half again as long!!

I got the message, immediately. That first year alone, I caught 500 trout on the original little gold Rapala. Everywhere we've fished in the meantime, we've had practically no trouble in taking trout on the Rapala and lake troll, consistently outfishing all other rigs on the lake. Here is that basic outfit. Rig it this way and catch lots of trout:

Beginning closest to the rod tip, I feel that a 10 pound test monofilament line is good for starters. It is tied directly to the lake

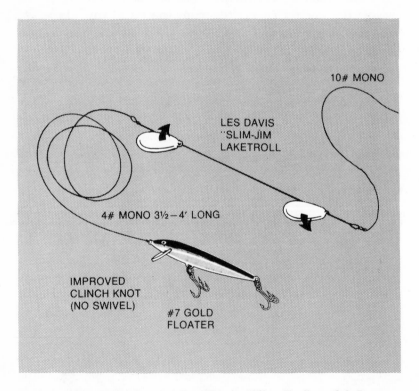

troll. I strongly prefer the Les Davis "Slim Jim" model. Its two, fluted contra-rotating blades (either all nickel, or half-brass, half-nickel) spin close to the shaft and thus minimize resistance and undue turbulence that might interfere with the action of the Rapala.

Fishing in The Pacific Northwest

I use 3½ to 4 feet of 4-pound test mono line between the lake troll and the #7 gold floating Rapala. I always tie the line directly to the eye of the lure with no intervening hardware. Any good knot will do: the Improved Clinch Knot, the Figure-Eight or the new "Uni"-Knot. Trim off the free end of the line *very close* to the Rapala and troll slowly with no additional lead if the rainbows in your lake or impoundment are at their habitual depths. We've also trolled the #7 floating Rapala with one or two split shot but *without* the lake troll in the same waters with good success, particularly East Lake here in Oregon and several lakes in British Columbia. Try both ways, to see which is better at producing fish. Whichever your technique, there is no lure for rainbows like the little #7 floating Rapala!

When the trout are down, as is so often the case with spooky German browns, some Oregon anglers use a lead-core line and enough weight to get the #9 or #11 floating Rapala down to the bottom. The secret is to let them float up a bit on three or four feet of light terminal leader ahead of the lure. This makes them less susceptible to hang-up than the counterpart Countdown Rapalas.

BROWN TROUT

I'm happy to report that there is increasing interest in brown trout out here. The centers of attention are on the upper reaches of one of the finest trout rivers in America, the Deschutes, and Wickiup Reservoir and Lake Lemolo, an impoundment on the upper Umpqua.

Anglers on the Deschutes usually begin with the #9 fluorescent red floating Rapala; again, tying the lure directly to an 8 or 10-pound monofilament line. The technique is not too difficult:

The cast is upstream and quartering in the relatively quiet runs and pools where the big but extremely cautious meat-eaters seek sanctuary. (There is no night fishing in Oregon. The law here requires us to stalk brown trout by day.) As the lure sweeps slowly downstream with the current, the angler begins a slow, even retrieve, *jerking* his rod periodically, as though setting the hook, with a pronounced bank-side motion. This kind of retrieve seems to make our big Deschutes browns go slightly crazy. Their favorite forage is crayfish, frogs, smaller fish, mice and even birds. The life-like action of that erratically swimming #9 fluorescent red floater entices them like no other artificial.

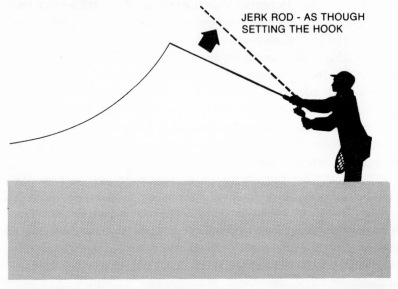

JERK ROD - AS THOUGH
SETTING THE HOOK

On the reservoirs and impoundments, most of the fishing for browns is as described above, with leaded lines and a floating Rapala kept free of the bottom by three or four feet of light mono tied directly to the lure. Again, the fluorescent red color seems to get the job done best.

DOLLY VARDENS

The Dolly Varden (strictly, not a trout, rather a western char) offers some tackle-busting action on the lower reservoirs of the Deschutes. Occasionally, these cannibals reach weights of over 20 pounds; however, the average is much lower. The Dolly Varden has an unfortunate fondness for young chinook salmon, so many kingfishers hate them with a passion. Stomach samples from a number of Dolly Vardens on our Imnaha River revealed an average of 5 to 12 chinook fingerlings being digested by each.

Be that as it may, the Rapala proves deadly to the Dolly Varden when fished where the stream enters the reservoirs of the lower Deschutes.

A lead, in the form of a bell sinker, should be heavy enough to take a three-way swivel rig to the bottom. A #7 or #9 Rapala (experiment to find the best color) should be tied directly to the three feet of light monofilament line connecting the lure to the swivel. Troll very slowly in the upper stretches of the reservoirs, where the fast water enters, permitting the lead to bounce the bottom and the Rapala to work like a forage fish. Big Dolly Varden mistake it for a minnow, providing slashing strikes and battles to the finish.

STEELHEAD

Ask anyone hereabouts the location of the Steelhead Kingdom and they'll reply, "the Pacific Northwest!" The steelhead *is* truly a kingly fish. This migratory, sea-run rainbow provides thrills without number. He is a worthy opponent for any angler.

It is my judgement that the steelhead provide us with the world's finest sportfishing, day-in, day-out, and most of it within an hour's drive of metropolitan Portland. Although the steelhead spends its ocean life at great distances from land, there is a constant migration back to the native rivers of the Oregon-Washington-British Columbia coast. It is a constant migration because groups of steelhead return every month of the year. There is no slack season.

The steelhead move into their native rivers in groups, migrating upstream via the identical routes, through each riffle and pool, that their ancestors have followed for generations before. They will rest in the same spots, bunch up in favorite holes and hold in a preferred area of a long riffle. Veteran steelheaders get to know these spots through long experience. Some can even read a strange river by its surface characteristics.

The Rapala Deep-Diver #90 has given less-experienced fisherman an instant tool that puts them more nearly into parity with the grizzled vets in the search for this marvelous fish. Unlike every other diving plug that I know, only the Deep-Diver #90 (or it smaller relative, the #70) works with consistent effectiveness through every inch of the retrieve. Other, less dependable divers must be checked frequently for correct action. But with the Deep-Diver, you *know* that it's always working right; always attracting fish rather than putting them off by virtue of some weird action.

Although we sometimes cast the Deep-Diver #90 from shore

or boat for steelhead, our most effective use of the lure involves slowly trolling back and forth *as we progress down the stream. Never troll upstream for steelhead.* The best stretches to troll are long, uniform flows of moderate speed, where the steelhead lie in the channel of the run; slicks above rapids, where the water seems to be gathering speed; and over submerged rocks, ledges and other structure offering cover.

When you're onto such a spot, tie the Deep-Diver #90 directly to your line. I recommend mono in the 8 to 15-pound range. Let the lure drift back from the boat for about 75 feet, at which point you stop playing out your line. Once your line is snubbed, the Deep-Diver will plunge, bounce and wobble to the bottom, sending out strong steelhead signals. Repeat: Work the boat slowly and gradually across and *down* the current, presenting the Rapala as

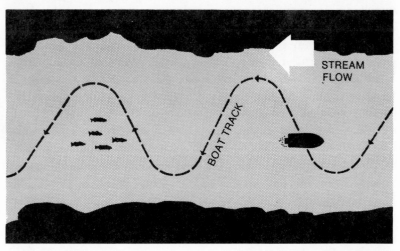

USE JUST ENOUGH FORWARD POWER FOR STEERAGE. BOAT DRIFTS STERN-FIRST DOWNSTREAM IN "SWEEPING" PATTERN

an on-coming, deep-diving target to the hungry steelhead moving inexorably up-river.

Steelhead seem to prefer different colors at different times and under different conditions. So it's best to experiment among the color options offered in the Deep-Diver series: silver, gold, blue or fluorescent red.

SALMON

The two major salmon species sought by gamefishermen of the Pacific Northwest are the chinook (or king) salmon and the coho (or silver) salmon. The most popular technique is trolling the ocean near the shore, in large protected bays or in the mouths of the large rivers. A rig I have used with some success consists of the following:

A 10 ounce mooching lead is tied to the line. A 40-inch monofilament leader of 30 to 40-pound test weight connects the lead to a size No. 0 Herring Dodger (again, I prefer the Les Davis product), with 28 inches of 30-pound test mono going from the Herring Dodger to the Rapala Deep-Diver #90. Using this rig for coho, we have trolled very successfully at a distance of only 10 to 15 feet behind the boat, practically in the prop-wash, moving much faster for this species than for the larger chinook. Although live bait is preferred by these two salmon, the Rapala Deep-Diver #90 is as effective as any plug for chinook and coho.

THE NON-SALMONIDS

Although the salmon-type species dominate our sport fishery, several other varities bear special mention. Striped bass in good numbers are found in the lower Coos River, the Umpqua and in the lower Coquille, usually from early spring until late fall.

Less numerous and concentrated than trout and salmon, stripers nevertheless provide some action on the larger size Rapalas, from the #9 on up. The larger members of this species are encountered in the deep holes on the rivers, where we prefer to troll for them or cast from a boat. My choice of a lure in these spots is the Magnum sinker #13.

Although Oregon is not noted for its warmwater fishery, many of our customers do pursue largemouth bass and annually there are reports of catches of these fish in the 10 pound class. One thing I have noted about our Rapala-using bass fishermen is their reports of an unusual number of "doubles"—two fish on the same Rapalas on the same cast. I have to chalk this down to much more than coincidence.

There is a well-defined pattern of Rapala use among these bass anglers. Despite our advice to start out with a larger lure, most begin with the #7 or #9 floating model. But then, as they gain in experience and confidence, they progress to the #11 and finally "graduate" to the #13. These highly-satisfied anglers report the best luck around stick-ups and other traditional bass cover on impoundments and the backwaters of the Columbia and Willamette Rivers. Smallmouth inhabit the Snake and Columbia down to the vicinity of the Dalles; and that species, too, is susceptible to all of the Rapalas, including the Deep-Diver #70 model.

CANADIAN FLY-IN FISHING

As an accommodation to my customers, I regularly sponsor fly-in trips to excellent trout and salmon lakes in the nearby Canadian province of British Columbia. This gives me the opportunity to wet a line with a lot of old friends and talk fishing with a lot of new ones. There are some fantastic Dolly Varden lakes in B.C. The local char are beautiful in color and have deep-red, delicious meat. They are an extremely spooky fish during the day. But in the evening, from 6:00 p.m. to dark, they readily inhale floating Rapalas fished close to the top of the water with a light lead. These fly-in lakes also yield nice rainbows to the Rapala-Slim Jim rig described at the beginning of this story.

It's been a pleasure to share my Rapala fishing secrets with you. When you're out Oregon way, stop into the Larry's Sport Center in either Oregon City or Gresham. We'll be glad to tell you whatever's new in angling here. And wherever *you* are, always take plenty of time to go fishing!!

BUCK ROGERS

A foremost outdoor writer, E.L. (Buck) Rogers is one of those fortunate men who has been able to meld his livelihood and hobby into an interesting, active and meaningful life. Vocationally, Buck is board chairman of Outdoors Incorporated of Columbia, Missouri, a leading advertising and public relations firm serving the outdoor recreational market. Avocationally, he is an expert angler whose exploits have been published in all of the leading fishing magazines.

These interests have lead him to zero in on some of the more exotic species among South of the Border gamefish. They include the peacock bass, a voracious feeder and stubborn fighter which seems to have great potential for domestic waters warmed by the discharge of power plants to temperatures which cannot be tolerated by our standard species. Who knows? In some future edition of this book, Buck may be writing on how to tame peacocks with the Rapala!

As befits a top advertising man, Buck demonstrates both his strong research bent and writing skills in the following article on fish release. It is a practice to be greatly encouraged. More and more anglers are releasing their catches alive, guaranteeing continued fine fishing. We hope that you are a releaser.

RELEASE YOUR CATCH ALIVE

The head of a national fishing organization recently announced that his tournament anglers release 11,171 bass during the period from March 1972 to January 1974, but no one can tell us how many of these fish actually lived to provide sport for some other angler.

Indian guides working out of some of the better Canadian fishing camps now reluctantly throw back some of their excess pike, but most of these fish are so maimed by rough handling that they do not survive.

Or, how about the millions of fishermen who keep everything they catch and cull out the smaller fish as they replace them with larger specimens? Most of these fish, which are released after excessive handling, are doomed as surely as those remaining on the stringer.

My point is this; it makes little sense to throw fish back to feed the turtles. Releasing a game fish to live and fight again is a great idea, but let's make sure the fish actually lives.

I first became aware of the seriousness of this problem while fishing with a Minnesota sportsman, Ray Ostrom. Ray had just gotten back from Great Bear Lake and expressed concern about the growing scarcity of trophy sized lake trout in those waters. My concern was for the growing shortage of big northern pike elsewhere in Canada, and the ill effects that increased fishing pressure was having on our largemouth bass. We agreed that mortality in released game fish might be more substantial than most of us think, and with Ray's help I set out to find out all I could about the subject. Six months later, and with the cooperation of 40 prominent biologists scattered around the country, I felt I had enough facts to write this article.

Today, most knowledgeable sportsmen realize that we must release an ever-growing percentage of the game fish we catch if we are to preserve quality fishing in our American lakes and streams. Professional bass fishermen and the promoters who sponsor their tournaments have finally recognized this fact, too. Today, as a result of public pressure, most bass fishing tournaments at least go through the motion of having their contestants release their catch. But, is this the solution to the problem?

My answer to that question is no.

Here's an example. Of the 1503 bass caught and released in a recent Toledo Bend tournament, 93 percent died immediately. After 14 days 70 percent of the remaining bass had died, and half of the few left were badly infected with bacteria. Biologists concluded that only 2 percent of the bass released in this tournament would have survived if released directly back in the lake.

On the other hand, we know that bass, any game fish, can survive and prosper if released properly. In one experiment using tagged fish, one bass has been caught and released an average of four times each season for the past several years.

The trick lies in knowing when and how to release a game fish, and that's what this article is all about.

The most common causes of mortality in released game fish are as follows:

1. Injury during the unhooking process.
2. Improper handling during the release process.
3. Disease resulting from the excessive removal of mucus.
4. Shock and stress as a result of the fight and the way the fish is handled.
5. Swim bladder injury resulting from too rapid a depth change.
6. Lactic acid build-up.

Factors such as lactic acid build-up and mortality as a result of shock and stress vary in significance from species to species and from one individual fish to another. In this respect, fish are like people. Some of us can run a hundred yards without even breathing hard. Others would drop over with a heart attack after such exertion.

The other four causes of mortality, which are by far the most significant, can be eliminated or sustantially reduced with proper procedures.

Playing A Fish

Proponents of stiff "worm rods" and line heavy enough to string up a felled whitetail have tried to build a case against light tackle by stating that the longer the fight, the more a fish suffers from stress and later runs a risk of lactic acid poisoning. But, I do not agree and I cannot find many experts who can back up that theory with facts. Does a fish experience more stress as a result of a long fight in which he has a good chance of winning? Or is the shock more severe if he is hauled unceremoniously into a boat and uses up his energy flopping around on the floor of a boat, or wriggling in the clutches of his captor. If landed in the latter manner, the average fish will be harder to unhook, it will remain out of the water longer, and certainly more mucous will be removed with excessive handling. Furthermore, if a fish is cranked up rapidly

from some depths it will also suffer some degree of swim bladder damage. Considering everything, it makes sense to match tackle with the size and species of fish being caught, and letting it expend its energy in the watery element in which it lives.

Landing Your Catch

The best way to land a fish is not to land it at all. If you can release your catch without removing it from the water the odds are almost 100 percent in favor of survival. To do this a landing net is mighty handy. With a net you can contain your catch and remove the hooks alongside the boat or certainly in a minimum of time if it is necessary to boat your fish. A net makes it easier to hold a fish for hook removal, and less protective mucous is removed in the process. If you don't have a net, get one. It's the most efficient tool for landing and releasing fish that I know of.

Another handy tool to use in the release of fish is a pair of long nosed pliers. With a pair of these pliers you can frequently grasp a hook and shake a fish loose without touching it with your hands.

If a fish is hooked too deeply for this maneuver and if you don't have a net, it then will be necessary to remove it from the water with your hands. In this respect the technique varies from species to species.

Bass and panfish are best handled with a firm grasp on the lower jaw. Toothed fish such as walleye, trout, and piranah can be landed and held effectively with a firm grasp of the back and gill covers. Heavy-toothed fish such as pike, muskie, and dorado should be landed and held with a forefinger in the gill opening. In such cases, do not touch or injure the gill rakers. Never land a pike or muskie by sticking a thumb and forefinger in the fish's eye sockets. This barbaric practice, common in the Canadian northwoods, usually injures the fish's eyesight to such an extent that it cannot survive.

Handle a fish with wet hands, and as little as possible, because any dry surface removes body mucous. Without this protective surface most fish are subject to bacterial attack which can be fatal.

A Fish Out of Water

Most fish cannot survive out of water very long. Fish breathe by absorbing oxygen from the water as it passes through their gills. Oxygen starvation commences immediately. Death by suffocation is the end result of prolonged exposure to the air.

This situation is further aggravated by warm temperatures. A fish is a cold blooded creature and its metabolism increases as the temperature of its surroundings increases. As this metabolic rate increases so does its consumption of oxygen. As a result, a northern pike taken from a cold Canadian lake can survive out of water longer than a largemouth bass hauled out of a Texas reservoir in mid-summer. In this case, oxygen starvation will commence in a matter of seconds, not minutes. If removed from the water, speed of release in warm water fish is essential for survival.

Removing The Hooks

More fish are killed as a result of injury from careless hook removal than from any other cause, so it is essential that attention be given to this subject. Each case is an individual one, but the following are a few guidelines:

1. As mentioned previously, use a pair of long nosed pliers. Research has proven this tool to be many times more efficient than a pair of clumsy fingers.
2. Fish hooked in the lips or outside jaw should be released without removal from the water. Grasp hook with your pliers and shake loose.
3. If the fish is hooked in the interior of the mouth, removal with a pair of pliers can usually be effected efficiently. Use special care if one of the hooks is embedded in the gills.
4. Single hooks embedded deep in the gullet or gills should not be removed. In these cases, clip the leader as close to the lips as possible and release the fish. Tests have proven that, in most cases, these will rust out or cyst over and the fish will survive. In contrast, an attempt to remove hooks in these areas is usually fatal to the fish.
5. A jug or a spoon hooked deep in the gill rakers can frequently be removed by the "back door method". To effect this technique, remove leader from the lure and extract it, hook first, through the gill covers.

Diagnosis For Release

When can you release a fish and when should you keep it? This is a decision which must be made with each catch, and it is one which will improve with practice.

As a rule of thumb, do not release a fish with bleeding or injured gills. Fish with such an injury usually will not survive.

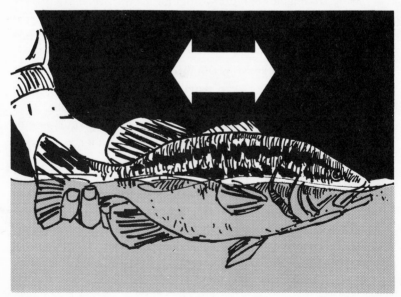

A fish that turns belly up, or floats on the surface when released probably will not "make it", either. In such cases, retain the fish or administer first aid to revive it. First aid is administered by holding the fish by the tail and gently moving it back and forth in the water. This technique forces water through the fish's gills and induces it to commence breathing again.

Usually, when a fish is strong enough to wriggle out of your grasp and swim away, it will survive. If a fish has not been injured, and it fights to get away, it is a candidate for release.

The Differences In Fish

Drag a catfish up on a gravel bar at night and it will still be alive and healthy the next morning. A bowfin or gar is equally hardy. The carp isn't far behind when it comes to surviving under adverse circumstances. But, as might be expected, our prized game fish are more delicate. Pike and other cold water fish, such as walleye, can tolerate a few minutes out of water. So can muskie, and trout taken from far north waters. Smallmouth bass have more staying power than its largemouth cousin, which cannot last very long out of water. Crappie and bluegill are in the same class.

One exception in the warm water game fish class is the peacock bass. According to Hawaii biologists, this exotic tropical gamester can take all kinds of abuse and still live. So, there's a difference in fish. The most critical from a release and survival standpoint are largemouth bass and panfish taken from warm water in hot weather.

Do's And Dont's

1. When fishing for fun, don't use killer baits such as live worms for trout, and small underwater lures for bass which are also swallowed deep.
2. Do use a landing net, especially for trout, long nosed pliers for all species, and jaw-spreaders for pike and walleye.
3. Don't attempt to remove a single hook buried deep in the body cavity. Cut the leader and release the fish with the hook untouched.
4. Don't release a fish which has injured, bleeding gills. This fish has little or no chance for survival.

5. Do try to unhook a fish to be released without removing it from the water. This technique can be improved with practice.
6. Don't keep a fish out of water one second longer than necessary. Remember, this time element is especially critical for bass and panfish when water and air temperatures are high.
7. Don't handle a fish to be released any more than necessary. Wet hands before handling.
8. Don't abandon a released fish it if appears to have trouble breathing or maintaining its balance in the water. Administer first aid until it has sufficient strength to swim away.
9. Do hold fish properly during the unhooking process. Example — grasp the lower jaw of a bass.
10. Do spread the word about the importance of this subject. For instance, the next time you see someone gouging a pike's eyes out, boot him out of the boat.

Do these things, and you, I, all of us will have better fishing for years to come. Fishing for fun is great sport, and it makes sense to release a portion or all of our catch. But, let's make sure that fish we release are alive and have a good chance of survival.

FISH FILLETING AND KNIFE CARE

FOR WALLEYE, TROUT AND FISH WITH SIMILAR BONE STRUCTURE.

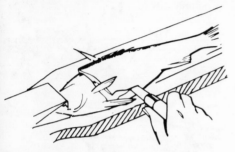

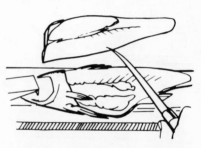

1. Make first cut just behind the gills. Slice down to the bone, then, without removing blade, turn it and slice straight along backbone . . .

2. . . . to the tail. Note that the fillet has been cut away from the rest of the fish. After slicing fillet off at tail, turn fish over and repeat procedure on the other side.

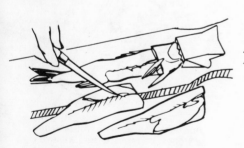

3. With both sides removed, you have cut away both fillets without disturbing fish's entrails. This is the neatest and fastest way to prepare fish. Now to finish the fillets . . .

4. Next step is to remove the rib section. Again, a sharp, flexible knife is important to avoid wasting meat. Insert blade close to rib bones and slice entire section away. This should be done before skin is removed to keep waste to a minimum.

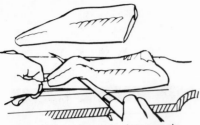

5. Removing the skin from each fillet is simply a matter of inserting the knife at the tail and "cutting" the meat from the skin. Start cut ½ inch from tail end of skin, allowing wedge for best grip. With the proper knife, like the "Fish 'N Fillet," it's easily done.

6. Here is each fillet, ready for the pan, or freezer, Note there is no waste. Remember not to overwash fillets. This will preserve tasty juices and keep meat in its firm natural state.

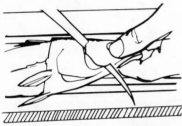

7. Cutting out the "cheeks" is the next important step. Few fishermen know that cheeks are the filet mignon of the fish. Though small, they're tasty and well worth saving.

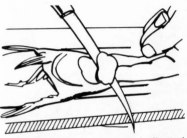

8. Slice into cheek where indicated then "scoop out" meat with blade, peeling away skin. Repeat on the other side. Many fishermen save cheeks until they have accumulated enough for a real gourmet's delight.

9. Here are all parts of the fish after you've finished. Note fish head, entrails, spine, tail and fins stay intact. This is the neatest way to prepare most game fish and, once you've mastered these few steps, the easiest.

10. Very large walleyes, like northern pike, contain troublesome Y bones. To remove from walleyes, with skin still on, run finger along lateral line of flesh side of fillet, feeling for tiny bones. When located, make wedge-shaped cut, as indicated, and lift out: Y bones will be inside. Then remove skin from other side of fillet. (#5 above).

FOR NORTHERN PIKE

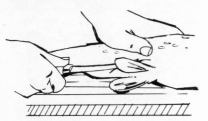

1. Remove two anal fins (ones ahead of tail) by running knife along each side of **outside** of fin base and attached heavy cartilage, pulling entire assembly free.

2. Fillet fish, with skin still attached, as for walleyes (#1 –#4). With fillet flesh-side up, make cut on angle along the pronounced lateral line. This is first step of removing tiny and troublesome Y bones.

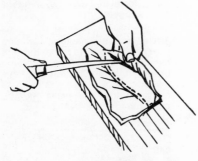

3. Fold over the flap, resulting from this incision and cut off all of flesh containing Y bones. Now remove skin from "deboned" fillet as for the walleye (#5).

FOR FISH WITH HEAVY RIB STRUCTURE:
LARGE BASS, PIKE OR SALT WATER SPECIES

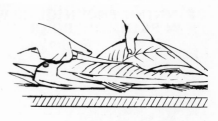

1. Holding head of fish firmly, make first cut at angle indicated, down to but **not** severing the backbone. Run knife at angle along backbone **without cutting through rib cage,** to point just behind vent, at which push blade all the way through and, with blade flat against backbone, run knife all the way to tail.

2. Holding free flap of meat aloft, carefully separate fillet from rib cage. Penetrate thin stomach skin to free fillet, turn fish over and repeat process. Now remove skin from outside fillets as for the walleye (#5).

189

Fish Filleting and Knife Care

FOR PANFISH TOO SMALL TO FILLET

Remove dorsal and anal fins by running knife point along each side of base and pulling free. This will remove many tiny bones from flesh. Scale fish, then behead, by cutting fish, then behead, by cutting body at an angle behind the gills. This will eliminate most of the rib cage and viscera. Finally, cut off the tail with two slanting incisions that will remove many fine bones.

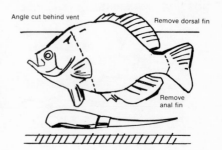

Angle cut behind vent

Remove dorsal fin

Remove anal fin

ADVANCE TIPS

1. Fish are like any other kind of food. Care must be given to preserve the flavor and keep them from spoiling. Most fish species should be cleaned and chilled as quickly as possible.

2. The juices in the flesh of a fish are much like that of good meat. They should be preserved to maintain peak flavor. If you wash your fillets, make certain the water is cold. Never overwash fillets. Avoid flooding meat with a hard-running hose. Many veteran fishermen dry the fillets with a cloth or paper towel and avoid washing the flesh altogether.

3. Get into the habit of cleaning your fish as soon as you're through fishing. Once you've mastered the proper filleting techniques, this takes only a few minutes. You conserve fish and make the trip more fun too.

4. Carry plastic bags for your fillets. One or two will neatly hold a day's catch. The plastic bags chill easily and hold in natural flavor and juices.

SKINNING TECHNIQUES WITH NORMARK SK-24 SKINNING BOARD

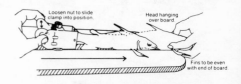

Loosen nut to slide clamp into position.

Head hanging over board

Fins to be even with end of board

Loosen knurled nut and slide into channel, keeping cone shaped piece on top side of groove. Use knurled nut to loosen and tighten for proper length of fish.

1. Place skin-type fish (catfish or bullhead) on board placing tail in clamp. Adjust for length of fish by loosening knurled nut on top of clamp and slide in slot until head of fish hangs over the end of the board and front fins (pectoral) are even with end of board. Then tighten knurled nut.

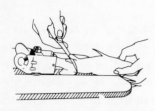

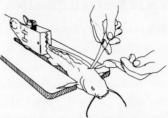

2. Start cut just behind rear dorsal fin at clamp and continue a shallow cut along the top of the fish to the back of the head.

3. Turn the blade and cut downwards to the backbone being careful not to cut through it.

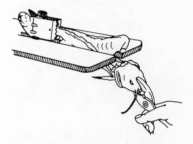

4. Place the board over the edge of table. Use a plier and grip the outside of the head. With the other hand, hold the board firmly.

5. Pull down on pliers, forcing the head below the board; and, as you pull, gently twist the head from side to side if necessary to keep skin separating evenly.

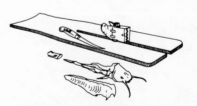

6. The head and skin will start to separate from the body taking with it the entrails and unedible parts of the fish. After skin is removed, fish is taken from clamp and tail is cut off.

7. Here are all the parts of the fish. The only thing left is to wash the body section lightly in cold water and prepare it with your favorite recipe.

The skin on catfish and bullheads will vary in thickness. This could cause the skin to tear prematurely. If this happens, it can be removed with pliers.

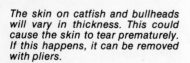

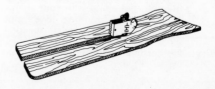

KNIFE SHARPENING

Whether you use a wet or dry stone is not as important as some say. You can get a good edge either way. Both water and oil help float away the metal particles and help bring up a finer edge than the dry method. Most sharpening experts say oil slows down the grinding process slightly, but insures a longer life for the stone.

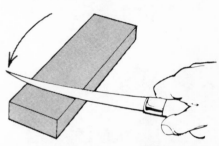

1. To sharpen knife like the Rapala Fish 'N Fillet, lay the blade edge on the stone at a 15° angle. Give each side of the knife about 10 strokes on the fine side of the stone. (If the knife is very dull, give each side of the blade five or six strokes on the coarse side of the stone first.)

2. Work the blade across the stone against the edge (as if cutting toward the stone). Don't press too hard or too light. A steady pressure with steady strokes will do it. Also be careful not to hold the knife too flat on the stone. This will result in a "feather edge" which wears down quickly.

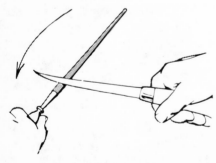

3. Setting the edge of your newly sharpened knife is very important. This is done with steel or strop bought right along with your sharpening stone. The steel does not sharpen your knife, but it realigns the microscopic teeth forming the cutting edge and revives its sharpness.

4. Using only light pressure, draw the blade toward you against the edge (as if slicing into the steel) from heel of knife to point. Knife's edge should be at about 20° (slightly greater angle for hunting knife). About ten strokes on each side of the knife is enough.

FREE FILMS FROM NORMARK

Listed below are ten 16 MM films—all produced in color, with optical sound track—covering various interesting kinds of fishing and designed specifically for audiences of all ages. The films are especially good for church and youth groups (Boy Scout troops, etc.), civic and service clubs, conservation and outdoor organizations, etc., because they are professionally produced, fast-paced and loaded with human interest as well as authentic fishing information.

Please note, however, that the films are for free distribution to *groups* rather than for individual viewing. In order to be fair to everyone, a fairly wide audience for each screening is sought.

At the end of the film listing is an order form that you can cut out or copy. All we ask is that you take good care of the film when it is in your possession and return it promptly to the Boyd Film Company after your viewing. Note, too, that we ask you to list both primary and alternate viewing dates.

MEX-BASS (26 Minutes)
Bass fishing thrills and the rugged beauty of Mexico is shown. Well known sport fishermen, Ron Weber, Bill Cullerton and Lew Childre, show various methods of fishing the bass from shallows to flooded-over frees. Very entertaining and informative.

SUMMER FISHING DREAMLAND (26 Minutes)
Two boys' fishing trip of a lifetime comes true when their uncles, Bill Cullerton and Ray Ostrom, take them to Lac La Ronge in Northern Saskatchewan, Canada. Their excitement will be felt by all, young and old, as they catch Northern Pike, Lake Trout and Walleyes. A good all-family film.

PANAMA "FISH BOWL OF THE PACIFIC" (26 Minutes)
Exciting trophy fish action from the blue waters of the Pacific, including the rare and colorful Rooster Fish. Famous sport fishermen, Ron Weber, Bill Cullerton and Leon Chandler, will show you these fish as well as the unexcelled splendor of this beautiful part of the world.

ALASKAN TROPHY TROUT (26 Minutes)
Well known sport anglers, Ron Weber, Leon Chandler and Bill Cullerton, take you to Iliamna (mother of the wind) country of Alaska. Join them in catching trophy rainbows and char against a background of unspoiled beauty. The scenes of giant brown bears, unbelievable fishing and rugged Alaskan wilderness will long be remembered.

COSTA RICAN TAIL WALKERS (26 Minutes)
Exciting pursuit story of trophy tarpon on light tackle in Costa Rican rivers. Well known sport fishermen, Ron Weber, Bill Cullerton, Tom McNally and Charlie Johnson, challenge each other for larger and larger tarpon. Shows spectacular jump scenes filmed on jungle rivers.

COHO CALLING (26 Minutes)
Shows the modern miracle of the transplanted Pacific salmon in the Great Lakes. Well known sport fishermen, Tom McNally, Bill Cullerton and Ray Ostrom, discuss the background of the coho and are shown catching the coho in lake, river and from the surf. Highly entertaining and informative.

MUSKIE CHASE (26 Minutes)
An unusual adventure film shot in the Lake of the Woods area of Canada. Excellent action of two nationally famous sport fishermen, Bill Cullerton and Ray Ostrom, chasing the elusive trophy fish and muskie. Highly entertaining, lots of action and very informative.

GOLDEN BASS (26 Minutes)
Takes place in the headwaters of the Amazon River in Colombia, South America. Bill Cullerton and Ray Ostrom find thrills and excitement in fighting the famous Tucanari Golden Bass. This beautiful tropical fish, which is shaped much like a North American largemouth bass, leads these two fishermen into adventure in the jungles of South America where other species add thrills and danger.

THE LAST LAUGH (26 Minutes)

Jack Crane and Buddy Upton are fishing pals who constantly argue about the best places and the best way to catch fish. Jack who owns a small tackle shop has been trying to convince Buddy to take a trip to the Ozarks, but Buddy argues there's better fishing right around home. One thing leads to another, and suddenly they've got a bet going. Join them and enjoy beautiful Ozark scenery, the spectacular fish action and discover who really has The Last Laugh.

BAJA FEVER (26 Minutes)

Sport fishing thrills at the tip of the Baja are shown to you by Ron Weber and Phil Greyshock. Filmed at Cabo San Lucas Mexico where the blue waters of the Pacific meets with the Sea of Cortes. Ron and Phil, well-known sport fishermen, will show you the elusive roosterfish, the acrobatics of the dolphin and billfish, and the speed of the wahoo. The rugged beauty of this land coupled with the excitement of its seas is truly a fishing adventure.

NAME OF FILM DESIRED _____

DATE WANTED _____/ ALTERNATE DATE _____

NAME OF ORGANIZATION _____

YOUR NAME _____ PHONE # _____

STREET ADDRESS _____

CITY_____ STATE _____ ZIP _____

FILL OUT AND SEND TO:
BOYD FILM COMPANY
1569 SELBY AVENUE ST. PAUL, MINNESOTA 55104 TELEPHONE: (612) 644-7317

HOW TO ORDER ADDITIONAL COPIES OF THE RAPALA FISHING GUIDE

Even the briefest examination reveals that almost every angler, even the most experienced, can have plenty to learn from "The Rapala Fishing Guide."

Order an extra copy for yourself — or send one to a fishing buddy or two. $3.95 price includes "The Rapala Fishing Guide," a Rapala fishing patch and the latest four-color Normark-Rapala brochure. The coupons below are for your convenience.

NORMARK CORP.
Department RFG
1710 E. 78th St.
Minneapolis, Minn. 55423
Here's $3.95. (Cash, check or money order.)
Send the works to:

(Name)

(Address)

(City)

(State)   (Zip Code)

NORMARK CORP.
Department RFG
1710 E. 78th St.
Minneapolis, Minn. 55423
Here's $3.95. (Cash, check or money order.)
Send the works to:

(Name)

(Address)

(City)

(State)   (Zip Code)

NORMARK CORP.
Department RFG
1710 E. 78th St.
Minneapolis, Minn. 55423
Here's $3.95. (Cash, check or money order.)
Send the works to:

(Name)

(Address)

(City)

(State)   (Zip Code)

NORMARK CORP.
Department RFG
1710 E. 78th St.
Minneapolis, Minn. 55423
Here's $3.95 (Cash, check or money order.)
Send the works to:

(Name)

(Address)

(City)

(State)   (Zip Code)

PRICE SUBJECT TO CHANGE WITHOUT NOTICE